By the same Author

A Guide to the General Assembly of
The Church of Scotland

A Guide to Congregational Affairs

A Guide to the Presbytery

A Guide to Ministerial Income

Kirk By Divine Right

A Guide to
The Ministry

ANDREW HERRON

THE SAINT ANDREW PRESS
EDINBURGH

First published in 1987 by
THE SAINT ANDREW PRESS
121 George Street, Edinburgh

Copyright © Andrew Herron 1987

ISBN 0 7152 0605 2

British Library Cataloguing in Publication Data

Herron, Andrew
  A guide to the ministry.
  1. Church of Scotland——Clergy——
  Appointment, call and election
  I. Title
  262′.1452411′023   BX9079

ISBN 0-7152-0605-2

Printed and bound in Great Britain by
Bell and Bain Limited, Glasgow.

Contents

Preface

Encouraged by the considerable interest which the other little *Guides* seem to have aroused I felt that perhaps the time had come to add a volume on the Ministry. This, when I got down to it, proved rather too vast a theme to encompass in a single booklet, so I have divided the material into two unequal parts: the former (and larger) deals with the question of how you go about entering the ministry, what you do (or, at least, ought to do) when you get there, and how you get out at the other end; and the latter (and smaller) has to do with the provision which is made for you throughout your ministry by way of stipend, manse, glebe (perhaps), expenses, and so on, and what you and your dependants may expect when the time comes for you to retire. The former I have called simply *A Guide to the Ministry*, while, for brevity's sake, I have entitled the latter *A Guide to Ministerial Income*.

In this first volume I have tried to deal quite fully and in detail with the whole compass of the minister's work, concentrating—I think properly —on the work of the parish minister, but not ignoring the increasing variety of other types of ministry.

Since the booklet is not intended as a legal text-book I have deliberately refrained from quoting at length from Acts, Regulations, Deliverances and the like, although I have generally tried to indicate where the appropriate authority may be found. I have permitted myself the luxury of writing fairly freely, flying the occasional kite, giving expression repeatedly to purely personal views, it being understood that the reader is completely free to disagree as violently as he will. The result is that the reader finds himself in the happy position of being able to cite me when he happens to agree with my views, and to say, 'Of course that's only Herron's idea', when he doesn't. I am not unaware that the horns of that particular dilemma can easily be turned!

My over-riding concern has been to make the booklet interesting and readable. With this in view I have in many instances probed a little into the historical background of some of the peculiar features of the ministry, and I have also drawn freely from my own experience of how the regulations have been found to work in practice. With more than half a century of the work of the ministry now behind me, I am more than ever convinced it is the most rewarding, and one of the most intensely interesting, occupations in which one could possibly be engaged. I have found a great deal of pleasure writing about it all: my hope is that you may find some comparable pleasure reading these pages.

I should like to acknowledge the help I have had from Mr Ronald Blakey who read over the whole work, commenting particularly, and most helpfully, on the material in the opening chapters, and also to Professor Robert Davidson, and Messrs Duncan M'Phee, Tom Kiltie and Thomas M Hunter for comments on the chapter on 'Other Appointments'.

Glasgow
September 1986   ANDREW HERRON

1

Preparing for the Ministry

Before dealing with the detail of how an aspirant to the ministry is to proceed, there are one or two preliminary matters which it will be an advantage to have cleared out of the way.

What is the Ministry?
For many generations this was a question to which an answer could easily be given, for the ministry of the Church of Scotland was characterised by two things: first an identity of function in that all ministers were doing essentially the same thing under very similar conditions (ministering to the spiritual needs of the people of a parish), and second by an equality in status. That situation is considerably changed today.

This is because the years since the Second World War have seen a wide diversification in the nature of the ministry, the parish ministry continuing more or less unchanged, but being supplemented by a variety of chaplaincies—to hospitals, universities, prisons, industry, as well as, of course, to the Forces—and also by Associate Ministries and by Community Ministries. So keen is the interest here that a Sub-Committee of Assembly exists specifically to deal with 'New Forms of Parish Ministry'.

And it is also because since 1981 we have had an Auxiliary Ministry, an unpaid ministry discharged on a part-time basis. The Auxiliary Minister enjoys equality with other ministers to the extent that his ordination is identical and his ministering is of identical effect. But it is quite unrealistic to suggest that a minister who cannot be inducted to a parish, and who may function only under the supervision of a full-time minister, enjoys equality of status with his supervisor. Even ignoring the question of equality, differences are so great that it will be easier for me to devote a separate chapter to the Auxiliary Ministry in all its aspects, proceeding meantime on the basis that we are thinking of how one is to prepare to enter upon the work of the full-time ministry.

Women and the Ministry

In common with medicine and the law the ministry was for long an exclusive male preserve. Attempts to change this pattern met with little success. And then in 1966 a first breach was made in the male defences with the passing of an Act which opened the eldership to women on the same terms as men. This stage had been reached only after a bitter struggle. As far back as the 1930s an effort to open this door had looked like proving successful, but the opponents of the change, alarmed that they were losing the support of the male-dominated Church courts, sought to call in the female reserves and were successful in having the matter sent down to congregations, which they were confident would throw it out, as indeed they did. To some it must have appeared that having an important issue remitted to congregations for determination represented a constitutional change far more revolutionary than having women admitted to the eldership; and to all it must have been apparent that there existed no proper machinery either for taking or for assessing the weight of popular opinion. As had been inevitable the move led to the matter being dropped for the time-being.

That the discussion often involved more prejudice than doctrine was illustrated, for me at least, when I was presented with a Kirk Session report prepared by an otherwise highly intelligent Session Clerk who wrote (of women in Kirk Sessions) — 'Those who have had experience of women in public affairs were unanimous in testifying that they either talk interminably and so keep the business back or they never open their mouths and so do not contribute to the business at all'. Not easy to know what the right thing is for a poor lassie to do, is it?

In 1964 the Panel on Doctrine presented a report on 'The Place of Women in the Church' and this was sent down to Presbyteries for consideration and comment. Presbyteries were not asked to vote on the various issues raised, but many did and the replies clearly indicated that opinion was heavily weighted in favour of the admission of women to Kirk Sessions and was almost equally divided over the question of women and the ministry. The Panel decided to leave aside for the present the latter question but to press on with the preparation of an Overture to go down under the Barrier Act, and this resulted in 1966 in the Act providing that 'women members of a congregation shall be eligible for ordination and admission as elders on the same terms and conditions as men members of a congregation'.

The doctrinal objections to the ordination of women being now out of the way it was as early as the following year that an Overture was sent down under the Barrier Act proposing to open the ministry to women on the same terms and conditions as men. This having gained the support of 42 Presbyteries to 17 (with two equally divided) the Assembly of 1968 passed the appropriate legislation.

Now, roughly 20 years on, a quick count indicates that there are 58 women ministers in the service of the Kirk: 45 inducted to parishes and 13 in other appointments (of whom 20 and 6 respectively are married women). The number is increasing steadily, if slowly, and in the year of writing, out of the 61 students licensed 14 were women.

A Question of Language – In its report to the Assembly of 1986 the Board of World Mission and Unity had much to say about 'choosing the right words' in Christian communication and the need 'to avoid the now archaic practice of using male language when the intention is to refer to all people'. A highly commendable sentiment. But anyone who has tried to frame legislation which is to apply equally across the sexes will quickly have discovered the inadequacies of the English language in this regard. The constant and dreary repetition of 'he or she', 'him or her', 'his or her' is the least of the difficulties confronting such an author. That is why in what follows I have chosen to write from the point of view of the male candidate (still very much the majority situation) with the note that suitable adjustment should be made where appropriate, and if this gives offence to any I can only express my regrets.

Sense of Vocation

Always it has been accepted that the ministry is more than just a profession, it is a calling. Whatever may at one time have been the case nobody today is likely to be lured into the ministry by the thought of its rich financial rewards. On the other hand, in a society where, for so many, work is a treadmill of meaningless repetition, the intimate personal relationships and the considerable job satisfaction which the ministry has to offer are not without their attraction. While, then, Presbyteries are constantly being exhorted to be diligent in recruitment, and while parish ministers are urged to bring the claims of the ministry consistently before bright young people in their congregations, one basic question in every case must be whether the prospective candidate has experienced a call to the ministry. In the absence of such a sense of vocation it is unlikely that anyone, however intellectually brilliant, will enjoy either a very happy or a very successful ministry.

In passing it might be said that the 'call' referred to in this context has to be distinguished clearly from the document presented by a congregation to the minister whom they have elected. I shall have more to say about that document in the proper place (*p* 83; in the meantime I want merely to point out that a call to the Parish of X and a call to the ministry are two entirely different things, if for no other reason than that while the one comes from a congregation, the other comes from God.

While, then, a sense of call is a 'must' for any prospective candidate for the ministry, there is more than that required—there has to be a profound grasp of the faith, a sympathetic understanding of other folk, a maturity of judgment, a fairly high level of general education, an ability to get along with others, some facility in communicating, and so on. Consequently, if you want to become a minister of the Church of Scotland you will normally fulfil your ambition by taking a fairly long and circuitous journey — you will begin as an applicant for recognition as a candidate, be selected as a candidate in training, attend classes as a student in a Faculty of Divinity, serve a period of training as a Probationer, and finally become eligible for election to a parish or for some other appointment. Your journey's end will not have been reached until through ordination you become a minister of the Church of Scotland. Divisions are necessarily arbitrary things, but I think it will be convenient to regard the stage of 'preparation' as ending at that point where the candidate becomes eligible for call.

Selection

The course of training is designed to supply and to foster those qualities and skills already referred to which are essential for the work of the ministry;

the initial selection is designed at once to test the sense of vocation and to identify those who seem ill-qualified to benefit from the course of training. The Presbytery has the responsibility of encouraging likely people to apply, but it is to the Assembly's Committee on Education for the Ministry that there has been entrusted the reponsibility for selection as well as for training—all in terms of Act V 1985, which replaced an earlier Act of 1973 as amended in 1980.

Committee on Education for the Ministry—This Committee forms a constituent element in the Board of Education and consists of a Convener, five Vice-Conveners, and 31 Members (all Assembly appointed), four Members appointed by the Divinity Faculties, and two representatives appointed by the parent Board. In addition there are Members without Voting Powers—the four Deans of the Faculties of Divinity, four Student Members, one Member from the Board of Ministry and Mission, and the Principal of the Episcopal Church College. There are Sectional Committees, those relevant to our present purpose which are called 'Recruitment and Selection', 'Supervision of Students' and 'Supervision of Probationers'. It will be convenient throughout this chapter to refer to the Committee on Education for the Ministry as 'the Committee'. All the main points in relation to training for the ministry are dealt with hereunder, but for those who wish further details, reference should be made to the *Church of Scotland Year-Book* for 1986 where at page 349 the Act is printed in full; or copies of the Act may be acquired from the Department of Education at 121 George Street, Edinburgh.

Acceptance for Training

Application—The first step along the way of
candidature is the submission to the Committee of
an application which has to reach them, not later
than 31 January of the year in which the applicant
hopes to begin his course. In fact two application
forms have to be completed, one going to the
Committee and the other to the Clerk of the
Presbytery of the applicant's place of residence or
of his congregational affiliation. The forms can be
obtained from the Secretary of the Committee at
121 George Street, Edinburgh. It is stated that the
two do not need to be completed 'in exactly the
same way, using the same words throughout'—
that is to say, there are two forms, not one form in
duplicate. The applicant must be already a communicant member of the Church of Scotland
(there are exceptions: for details of which see
Paragraph 2 of the Act). An applicant cannot
attend Selection School in advance of his eighteenth birthday, and at the opposite extreme an
application will not be entertained from anyone
who by 30 September in the year in which he will
begin his course will have attained the age of 58
years. Once accepted an applicant has to begin his
course within three years, otherwise the acceptance
will lapse.

Candidature—The Presbytery which has received
the application has the duty of transmitting to the
Committee, in writing, comments on the character,
beliefs, vocation, motivation, and general suitability of the applicant, and will therefore want to
interview him. A complication can arise at this
stage in the case of an applicant presently in

secular employment in that his position and prospects therein may be gravely prejudiced if it becomes known that he has it in mind to leave in order to enter the ministry. It is important therefore that the fullest confidentiality be observed. It is suggested that when it deals with the report on the interview the Presbytery should meet in private, or, better still, that it should remit to a committee to carry through the interview and prepare the report, giving authority for this to be transmitted direct without being submitted to a meeting of the full court. While this latter method has much to commend it, wise judgment must be exercised. A very awkward situation arose when such a committee, in name of the Presbytery, recommended nomination of a candidate whose personal record was such as to raise a most serious question of principle, the facts not having been disclosed to the Presbytery. In such circumstances the Committee, even if vested with full power, should certainly take the whole Presbytery into its confidence — meeting in private, of course.

The Committee being satisfied with the written report supplied by the Presbytery, and being satisfied too on its own observation that the candidate does not suffer from any obvious disqualification, will arrange for him to attend a Selection School.

Selection School

The idea of employing the medium of the Selection School for the sifting of candidates for the ministry was first advanced in the Report of the

Committee in 1966 when it was argued that there was need for 'a more effective method of detecting the less suitable candidates'. An experiment was conducted at St Andrews over a period of rather more than a full day, ten applicants being assessed in two groups by a total of six assessors in an extended-interview situation involving discussion as well as *viva voce* and written tests. Following upon the success of this experiment it was recommended to, and agreed by, the Assembly of 1967 that the principle of the Selection School should be adopted. The following year it was reported that five further schools had been held, the length of the session having been extended to two full days and the procedure followed having been an adaptation of that of the Civil Service Selection Board and having included such down-to-earth exercises as writing a tactful reply to a 'difficult' letter of the kind that might be encountered in a typical parish situation. Though the subjects covered were wide and varied, an assurance was given that assessment was based on the applicant's overall performance.

In 1984 the matters of the selection of candidates and of the role the Presbytery should play in their promotion and in the care of them at all stages was remitted for fresh consideration to the Committee which in turn appointed a Special Review Committee to carry out this task. A very full report was submitted to the Assembly in 1985. In general terms the Review Committee came to the conclusion that a centralised selection system was much to be favoured and that the Selection School system was working well. At the same time certain changes in detail were effected as a consequence of the investigations.

Assessors—Presbyteries were, in 1985, invited to submit names of personnel—ministerial and lay, male and female—thought by them suitable to act as assessors, and they may be asked to do this again as the need arises. The actual appointing is done by the Committee, and for this they are answerable only to the Assembly. Assessors serve for a period of not more than six years after which they withdraw for at least two years before becoming eligible for re-appointment—and then only for a maximum of one further term. The same time-limits apply in the case of Directors of Selection Schools —although to these rules there are certain exceptions set forth at length in the Report.

Object of Assessment—The purpose of the Selection School is to attempt an assessment of the applicant's overall suitability, taking into account— all within the context of full-time ministry—such factors as a sense of vocation, an understanding of the faith, maturity, personality, commitment, powers of communication, ability to relate to other people, ability to study, leadership, age and health. And presumably anything else considered relevant!

Recruitment and Selection Committee—This Sectional Committee consists of 13 persons chosen by the Committee from within its own Assembly-appointed membership along with the four Principals of the Colleges (or their nominees) and one representative from the Board of Ministry and Mission, and it is the body which has to reach a decision in respect of every applicant. To assist them in so doing the members have in their hands the full report and recommendations of the assessors from the Selection School, and there are also available all other papers in the case. The Committee may decide to accept the candidate, in which case it will prescribe an appropriate course of training for him and will instruct him forthwith to seek nomination by his Presbytery. On the other hand it may decide not to accept the applicant, in which case it will inform him that it is open to him to return to a second Selection School and, as necessary or desired, to a third. Indeed an applicant may have a fourth 'try', but that only on application to the Committee itself. Normally there must be a 12 month gap between appearances at Selection School, and at each fresh appearance the applicant will be in the hands of assessors who have not previously met him and who have no access to the reports of his earlier appearances. In cases where the Selection School report does not recommend acceptance it should wherever possible include a paragraph making specific comment on the applicant's future involvement in Christian witness as that appears to the assessors.

Counselling–Because the ministry is a calling, and because the applicant may have a particularly strong sense of vocation, the experience of being turned down in this way can be a quite traumatic one calling for careful pastoral attention. As he sees it, he is here offering his life to Christ, and all the Church has to say is 'no thank you'. His faith may have taken a heavy knock. He may be feeling very bitter. And so, in the letter conveying to the applicant a negative decision, there is a note included saying that he may expect to hear fairly soon from a counsellor appointed to act in his case. The first approach from the counsellor will take the form of a letter offering his services in this capacity but at the same time making clear that the applicant is under no obligation to accept. The counsellor will be afforded access to the report of the assessors, but this he must not, in any circumstances, disclose to the applicant. Neither must the counsellor be regarded as a coach to train the applicant for his next appearance at Selection School. The function of the counsellor is to be a friend to the disappointed man, to lend a listening ear and, as far as possible, to help him to come to terms with the decision reached and to shape his future in the light of it. Real advantage could well accrue from the applicant's own minister coming in at this stage and in some circumstances a meeting of all three could prove most beneficial.

A Difficulty—A weakness of the system lies in the fact that while the Church can delay recognising a student as being in training for its ministry, it cannot prevent him—given that he has the necessary academic qualifications—from studying in a Faculty of Divinity. So he enrols and takes first-year classes. Let it be that he is accepted at his next appearance at Selection School; he has avoided the loss of a complete year on his road to the ministry—and who would blame him for wanting to do this? If, however, he is still not accepted, what then? He may go on hopefully to take another year's classes; and so on until he has completed the entire University course—possibly with a lot of distinction—but he has now had his final rejection as a candidate in training. A desperately unhappy human situation can emerge. When it becomes clear that this kind of situation is building up—as often it can be very clear—counsellor and parish minister have a particularly heavy responsibility to try to persuade the student that his undoubted gifts and dedication can and should be put to other uses. God may be served in many ways besides the ministry, although when a man has set his heart on the ministry it can be hard to convince him of this.

Review of Decision—An unsuccessful applicant may appeal to, and be heard before, the Sectional Committee, stating why he is convinced he had less than a fair hearing at the Selection School. He may, for example, point to procedural irregularities which he alleges occurred there and which he contends militated against him, or he may claim that for personal or family reasons he was under unusual strain at the time and so unable to do himself justice. Should he so desire, he may be accompanied at the hearing by an Observer of his own choosing, but such an Observer has no right to take any part in the proceedings and is given no access to confidential documents. Having heard the applicant, the Sectional Committee has a choice of three courses: (a) it can adhere to its original decision; (b) it can resolve to reverse its original decision and accept the applicant; or (c) it can uphold the appeal to the extent of making it possible for the applicant to come up anew at the earliest possible Selection School where he will be seen by a different group of assessors; and if this is done then for the purpose of calculating the total number of possible appearances, the School, whose decision has been successfully appealed against, will not be included.

If the review procedure outlined above leaves

the applicant still dissatisfied he may appeal to the parent Committee (on Education for the Ministry) which will itself hear his case. For the purpose of such a hearing those involved in the affair at any of its earlier stages will not sit with the Committee. Those who are to judge the appeal will receive copies of the Selection Board report and will consider also any material supplied by the appellant either in writing or in person. The same three options will be open as above, and the right to be accompanied by an Observer will also apply.

Petition to Assembly—If still dissatisfied at this stage the applicant has the right to appeal to Caesar—he can petition the General Assembly craving that they will instruct their Committee on Education for the Ministry to accept him as a candidate in training for the ministry. The report points out that in any such process the full Selection School papers—with all their highly personal details—will have to be circulated to all the Assembly commissioners, and it has also to be borne in mind that the considerable expense of all this printing will fall upon the petitioner.

The Candidate

Nomination by Presbytery—The applicant who, having passed through Selection School, has been accepted by the Selection Committee, has now, in terms of the Act, achieved the status of a 'prospective candidate'. It is at this point that he may be nominated by his Presbytery which will normally be the Presbytery within which the congregation of which he is a member is situated, and he should make written application to that Presbytery through its Clerk. A prospective candidate who has been refused nomination by one Presbytery is expressly barred from making application for nomination by another without the prior written approval of the Committee, which has to satisfy itself that such an application is 'in the best interests of the Church'.

Types of Candidate—Once nominated by the Presbytery the 'prospective candidate' becomes the 'candidate' and will belong to one or other of three categories:

(1) Ordinary Candidate: being a person under the age of 23 on 30 September in the year when he begins, or is deemed to have begun, his prescribed course. To be accepted such a candidate must possess passes in Higher and Ordinary Grade examinations (or their equivalent) sufficient to qualify him for admission to University, and if these qualifications are such as to enter a Faculty other than Divinity he will be encouraged to take the Regular Course.

(2) Mature Candidate: being a person over 23 but under 40 on 30 September as above. To be accepted for the appropriate course (a first BD) he must fulfil the requirements for admission to a Faculty of Divinity, but in the case where his qualifications entitle him to enter upon a two-degree course he too is to be encouraged to take the Regular Course.

(3) Older Candidate: being a person over 40 but under 58 on 30 September as above. To be accepted he must have good educational qualifications or recognised professional or vocational experience as deemed satisfactory by the Committee.

General Requirements—Each candidate, before his course can be recognised, has to have passed three examinations in Bible Knowledge. Also, each candidate in the course of his theological study has to engage in three periods of practical work prescribed by the Committee. In any case where the latter is not done, or having been done is not sustained, the Committee will prescribe a Probationary Period extending up to two years.

Courses of Study

There are three normal courses of study, all of which include the following subjects: (a) the interpretation and use of Holy Scripture, of both Old and New Testaments; (b) the development and growth of the Church, including special reference to the Church of Scotland; (c) the principal doctrines of the Christian faith, their interpretation, defence and application; (d) the principles of Christian Ethics; and (e) the practice of the ministry, attention being given to public worship, the sacraments and preaching, the pastoral ministry, Christian education, pastoral discipline, Church law and procedure, and speech training.

The Regular Course—This consists of a First Degree in Arts, Social Science, Medicine, Science, Music, or Law, or any other such Degree as may be accepted as qualifying the applicant to study for the Bachelor of Divinity degree in one of the four older Scottish Universities, followed by a course of not less than three years of study leading to the BD degree. A candidate who contrives to complete both degree courses within five years will be required to take one further year's study unless he had attained the age of 23 before beginning the latter of the two courses.

The Alternative Course – This consists of four years of study leading to the attainment of the BD as a first degree and has to be followed by two years of further study at University level as determined by the Committee not later than the end of the third year of the course. In the case of a student who had reached the age of 23 by the time he began the BD part of the course only one year of further study will be demanded.

The Mature Candidate's Course – This consists of a three year course wholly within the Faculty of Divinity leading to the attainment of the Licentiate in Theology (LTh) qualification and has to be followed by two years of study for a Diploma or a Certificate in Ministry or Pastoral Studies; or by such other course as may be approved by the Committee.

Special Courses – In the case of a person with a first degree other than a BD (for example, a Bachelor of Theology or Master of Theology) from a Faculty of Divinity in Scotland, or with a theological degree from a University furth of Scotland, the Committee is to consider the course to be taken in light of the whole circumstances of his case. Only in the most exceptional circumstances will the Committee prescribe a Special Course for a candidate under the age of 40.

There is also on offer to older candidates (usually not under the age of 50) a Special Two-Year Non-Graduating Course particulars of which may be obtained from the Secretary of the Committee at 121 George Street.

Supervision

The supervision of candidates is a duty shared between the Committee and the Presbytery.

Liaison Committees—There are four of these (one connected with each of the Universities) and they consist of representatives of the Sectional Committee on the Supervision of Students, the College Principal with appropriate members of staff, and representatives appointed by neighbouring Presbyteries and Synods, and they advise the Committee on all matters relating to candidates and their progress towards the successful completion of their prescribed courses. When a Liaison Committee becomes aware of significant difficulties affecting a candidate it informs the Committee which in turn communicates with the Presbytery.

Sectional Committee on the Supervision of Students—This consists of 11 members drawn from the main Committee, the four Principals of the Colleges (or their nominees) and the four Student Members from the main Committee (or their alternates)—19 in all—and, as its name implies, it is responsible for the overseeing of candidates from their being accepted as students until they are licensed.

The Presbytery—Throughout the whole of his course the candidate remains under the pastoral supervision of the Presbytery which nominated him, unless during the period he has moved his residence, in which case he must, within two months of moving, submit to the Clerk of the Presbytery which nominated him written notice that he wishes to be transferred, whereupon the latter will furnish him with a Certificate which he must immediately lodge with the Clerk of the Presbytery to which he has moved.

Presbyteries are required to confer at least once a year with candidates under their care, and, to assist them in this, they are, not later than 25 July, to be supplied by the Committee with a report relating to progress during the previous academic year. The Presbytery has thereafter to satisfy itself as to the candidate's fitness to continue and must intimate its decision to the Committee not later than 25 September. The Presbytery has power, after conference with the Committee, to suspend or terminate a person's candidature, and in such a case the Presbytery's decision is final, subject, however, to the right of the candidate to petition the General Assembly for a review of his case. This would appear to me to mean that if the Presbytery terminated a man's candidature that judgment would immediately become operative, and if he wished to petition he would have to crave to be reinstated.

I can find no authority for this, but I am clearly of the opinion that if a candidate has been guilty of some grave moral lapse it is for the Committee, in consultation with the Presbytery, to consider his position relative to his candidature and if this were to be terminated it would be as the result of a judgment of Presbytery. The actual exercise of discipline, however, I would take to be the affair of the Kirk Session of the congregation to which he belongs, the responsibility for pastoral care lying with the minister of that congregation. Only after licence does he come under the discipline of the Presbytery.

Licence

Candidates entering their final year are, not later than 31 October, to inform the Committee to which Presbytery they intend to apply for licence, and they are, not later than the end of the following month, to make such application to their supervising Presbytery. The Committee is to prepare a full list of all such proposed applications and to circulate a copy thereof not later than December to all of the Presbyteries of the Church stating that the Presbyteries concerned may take these candidates on trials and, subject to their courses being sustained, may license them, but without prejudice to the right of any other Presbytery to raise objection in the case of any one of them.

Objection—This covering letter indicates also that the Presbytery is at liberty to object to any candidate, whose name appears on the list, being taken on trials, and that if this is to be done the supervising Presbytery must be informed not later than 15 March. Commissioners may be appointed to prosecute the objection before that Presbytery. Since it will normally be the character, conduct, doctrine or ability of the candidate that is in question, it would seem to me that he should be cited and be at the bar for his interest and that the matter should be dealt with in private. The Presbytery having heard the objection may dismiss it and proceed with the trials; or it may decide to sustain it and not to proceed; or it may decide to refer the matter to the General Assembly. Since the Act does not specifically confer upon the Presbytery finality of judgment in this matter, the normal right of appeal (to the Synod) will lie with both the applicant and the objecting Presbytery; and any member of the supervising Presbytery may dissent and complain. Until such appeal has been disposed of no steps can be taken towards licensing.

Late Application—Where timeous application has not been made, a Presbytery may, if satisfied there has been good reason for the delay, proceed towards taking the candidate on trials, but it must first circulate information to all the Presbyteries of the Church setting forth the candidate's name and particulars and calling for objections to be lodged within three calendar months, the expense of the exercise being borne by the candidate. In a case where the lateness has been caused by the Committee having abbreviated the candidate's course, the procedure is as above but the expense is met by the Committee.

Trials for Licence—The candidate may be taken on trials for licence any time after 1 January following receipt of his application. The object of the trials is to enable the Presbytery to discover whether the applicant is 'acquainted with the present legal and sacramental practice and traditions of the Church of Scotland, and that he is a fit person to proceed to its ministry'. They consist of (a) an examination, which may be oral or written or both, on the principles and practice of the Church, and (b) the conduct of public worship at a principal service, in the presence of two ministers and two elders from the Presbytery. A meeting is then held of those who have supervised the course, the examiners in (a) above, and those who were present at the service in (b) above—and a decision is reached as to whether or not to recommend that the trials be sustained. All this may be done although the Presbytery is not yet in a position to license.

Service of Licensing—The actual Service of Licensing of a Student may not take place until the Presbytery has received from the Committee an Exit Certificate in his favour, has sustained his trials, and has made known to him in detail the vows he will be required to take. The Exit Certificate is a document stating that the requirements of the course have been completed to the satisfaction of the authorities—that is, that the necessary standards have been achieved in the relevant classes, that the Bible Examinations have been duly passed, and that the periods of practical work have been performed or that alternative acceptable arrangement has been made.

The Service will normally be held on a weeknight in a suitable church within the bounds, although if there is only one candidate the Service may appropriately be held in the church with which he is associated and may take place on a Sunday evening. In the course of the Service the Moderator will read the Preamble and put to the candidates the appointed questions, after which they will be required to sign the Formula. After the Service each licentiate is furnished with an extract of his licence, and it is customary in the course of the Service for the Moderator to hand over to him a copy of the Scriptures which he is being authorised to 'open' to the people.

Question of Timing—Because of the dates of the Faculty examinations the necessary information to enable the issue of Exit Certificates is not available until the closing days of June. This creates a difficulty for Presbyteries in the matter of holding the Service of Licensing. If, as I am contending in the next paragraph, one of the main purposes of licensing is to mark in quite bold and significant fashion the transition from divinity student to minister, then clearly it is important that the service should take place as near to the moment of transition as possible. The imminence of holidays and other summer commitments means this must be in the opening days of July, and this represents a very tight schedule. It is therefore common for Presbyteries to fix an *in hunc effectum* meeting for the Service of Licensing, but to do so 'subject to the necessary certification in the case of Mr AB being received by that date'. This suffers from the obvious disadvantage that if, for any reason whatever, Mr AB's Exit Certificate is not in the hands of the Presbytery Clerk, his licensing cannot proceed—with a lot of embarrassment for all concerned. For this reason some Presbyteries have been delaying the licensing until early September with the result that some students (for officially that is what they must still be called) begin their Probationary Assistantships without being Probationers. That does not unduly worry me, but I still feel strongly that a Service to mark an event loses a great deal if it is not held until the event is already months past.

Purpose of Licensing—The extract minute referred to above will, after narrating the circumstances, declare that 'the said Mr AB was licensed to preach the Gospel of the Lord Jesus Christ and to exercise his gifts as a Probationer for the Holy Ministry'. In regard to this—and indeed, in regard to the relevance of licensing in general—two questions have of late been raised: first a question asked by the Panel on Doctrine—whether it is sound theology to license for the preaching of the Gospel while withholding the right to dispense the Sacraments of the Gospel—and second, and more cogently, whether it is not something of a nonsense to authorise, as preachers of the Gospel, people who for years have, without let or hindrance, been occupying pulpits in the full knowledge of the Church. It was not always so. Writing a century ago, Mair in his *Digest of Church Laws* has these sharp comments to offer: 'Ministers are expressly prohibited from giving countenance or permission to students to engage in the public ministry of the Word before being regularly licensed to preach the Gospel. Hitherto the Church has considered that on the one hand the conduct of public worship was a service not to be grasped at, or even undertaken, immaturely, and that on the other hand the time and power of students was required for, and ought to be devoted to, their own studies. It is remarkable that in these days, when the field of study is so much enlarged, and the need for it so much greater, there should appear an inclination to permit, and even to encourage, students to leave their work and hasten to the pulpit'.

Whatever one may think of Mair's strictures the

fact has to be accepted that today the candidate has been permitted, indeed encouraged, to preach, and so to that extent the authority given at licensing is meaningless. The business of 'exercising his gifts as a Probationer for the Holy Ministry' is, however, as relevant as ever. In any case it is surely a good thing to mark in some significant way the passing of so important a milestone on the road towards the ministry.

Immediately after the Service, the Licentiate becomes entitled to wear the traditional clerical collar and to be designated as 'Reverend'. I am not aware of any law, civil or ecclesiastical, governing these matters of dress and address, but the foregoing certainly represents accepted practice within the Kirk, and I imagine that a Presbytery, if it were so minded, could instruct a Student, for example, not to call himself 'Reverend' and could take action against him for contumacy were he flagrantly to disobey.

Licentiates and Probationers

In consequence of the Service of Licensing our Candidate has now become a 'Licentiate' and the way lies open for him to become a 'Probationer'. For a long time these two terms were interchangeable, other synonyms in earlier usage having been 'Preacher of the Gospel' and the rather delightful 'Expectant'. Of recent years the custom has increasingly been adopted of using the term 'licentiate' to refer to one who has been licensed and is content to leave it at that, having no immediate intention of moving on towards ordination, whereas 'probationer' is used to designate one whose intention it is to move directly towards the exercise of a ministry, whether or not his period of compulsory service has been completed. The terminology has now, however, been given statutory definition (see hereunder) in terms of the Act of 1985 anent Students, Probationers, Licentiates and the Transference of Ministers, and I shall try to adhere to these terms.

At this stage the licentiate—by whatever name—is moving out of the control of one Committee into that of another and for a period he has responsibilities towards both; a situation which he can find quite confusing. He remains, however, under the supervision of the Presbytery which licensed him, and if he were to be alleged guilty of some moral fault it would be to that Presbytery, and no longer to his Kirk Session, that he would have to give account. Incidentally, if he were found guilty and deprived of his status, the technical term for the sentence would be that he had been 'silenced' — a peculiarly appropriate term for a Preacher!

Definitions—The 1985 Act referred to above opens with a list of 'interpretations'. A Probationer is defined as a Student (he was defined as a Candidate in the other Act) who has been licensed by his Presbytery and who is performing his Probationary Period. For a Licentiate on the other hand three separate criteria are given—he is (a) a Probationer whose period of service has been sustained, (b) a Student who has been exempted from the performance of a Probationary Period and has been licensed, and (c) a Student who, having completed his course and having been licensed, has not proceeded to the performance of a Probationary Period. That is to say, a Licentiate may be either someone who is now ready to be called to a charge or someone who has no interest in being so called, and who in any case could not be so called. Considerable confusion seems likely to arise when two so completely different classes should thus share the common title of Licentiate. To me it also seems unfortunate that the term 'Probationer' should be tied to the time of serving the compulsory period. If you are exempted from this then you never have the satisfaction of saying you are a Probationer.

Transition—The aspirant for the ministry is at this point, as has been said, in a state of transition, passing from the control of the Committee on Education for the Ministry to that of the Committee on Probationers and Transference and Admission of Ministers. Those licentiates who elect not to serve a Probationary Period continue in the care of the Education for the Ministry Committee to the extent that they cannot be inducted to a charge until that body has either prescribed and sustained, or has granted exemption from, a Probationary Period. It is expressly provided that those who have undergone such a period are given a certificate sustaining that period, and thereupon they pass completely from the control of the Education for the Ministry Committee; and this may be presumed to apply also where, in exceptional circumstances, exemption from the Probationary Period has been granted.

Roll of Probationers and Licentiates—Presbytery Clerks are, without delay, to forward to the

Committee on Probationers and Transference and Admission of Ministers (referred to throughout this section as the 'Probationers' Committee') particulars of all students who have been licensed, and the Secretary of the Committee is to send each for completion a form in which *inter alia* he is to indicate the kind of ministry he wants to pursue. Only after receipt of this form will his name be entered on the Roll which the Committee is obliged to keep.

Probationary Period—In days past some men on being licensed sought an assistantship where they might remain for one, two or even three years, while others immediately sought a parish of their own. The choice lay with the Probationer concerned. The year 1973 saw a radical change here, for at that time there was introduced the principle of a compulsory period of probation. It is said that the purpose of the Probationary Period is to provide a prolonged and intensive period of practical training and experience for candidates for the ministry, to complement the academic training provided and experience gained in attachments and assistantships during the University course, and to form an immediate preparation for the parish ministry.

Exemption—The Act said that the Committee would have power in special cases to grant exemption, and in the early days such exemptions were fairly freely given, it being accepted that a person of considerable experience in the world of affairs did not require any specialised training to equip him for the work of a parish. Soon, however, it became apparent that maturity in running a secular business or adroitness in holding a high managerial post can be more of a hindrance than a help in conducting the affairs of a parish, with the result that in recent times the whole system has been considerably tightened up so that today exemption is very much the exception.

Length of Service—Before becoming eligible to be elected to a home charge, a Licentiate must have served a Probationary Period at the direction and under the supervision of the Committee. The length of the Probationary Period is from eight to 12 months. If, as is customary, it begins between April and September it will run to 30 April of the following year; if it starts at any other time it will run for eight months at least. If the candidate has not performed the practical work prescribed during his course, an additional 12 months' probation will be demanded. The period is to be served in full-time employment (usually in a parish assistantship), and Presbyteries are by 30 May in each year to submit to the Committee a list of charges wherein suitable training can be received.

Certificate of Entitlement—At the same time that the Exit Certificate is issued, the candidate receives from the Committee a Certificate of Entitlement to undertake a Probationary Period, and this he must lodge with the Clerk of the Presbytery within whose bounds he is to be working, and that particular Presbytery thereupon assumes responsibility for him. A note of Certificates so issued is also sent to the Presbytery Clerk. It is in order for the Committee, after consultation with the Probationer, with the Minister and Kirk Session of the charge where he is working, and with the

Presbytery, to resolve to remove a Probationer or to make alternative arrangements for his placement during the remainder of his period. The Committee has power also to prescribe supplementary training.

While serving his period the Probationer is at liberty to give pulpit supply in vacant charges, but in no such case will he be eligible to receive a call to the charge concerned.

In February reports are received both from the Probationers and from the ministers under whom they are serving, and the Committee determines in each case whether the period is to be sustained. If the decision is favourable the Probationer is given an appropriate certificate, the Probationers' Committee is informed and the person becomes eligible for election and appointment to a home charge. He may not, however, be inducted to such a charge until he has completed the full Probationary Period. If the decision is unfavourable a further Probationary Period may be prescribed, almost certainly in another appointment.

Salary and Expenses

In 1974 the Assembly approved regulations governing the salary and expenses of Probationers, and these have since been adjusted from time to time. The position at time of writing is that the rate of salary is 75 per cent of the Minimum Stipend current during the year in which the Period began and remaining constant at that figure for the whole year; and if after his period has been sustained the Probationer continues beyond 12 months (whether or not ordained) the rate increases to 80 per cent of the Minimum for that year. It is important to note that no central funding is available after the first 12 months, and a second year can be undertaken only if the congregation is able and prepared to meet the total cost. Occupancy of a house or flat free of rent and rates is given, or payment of £750 per annum in lieu. (A Probationer in receipt of this sum must return it for Income Tax.) If a removal of household effects is involved, the reasonable cost of this is met. Travelling expenses, duly vouched, are met on the basis of 25p per mile for the first 4500 miles, 18p for the next 3000, and 12p thereafter. A motorcycle qualifies at half the rate for a car. Up to £400 may be paid for necessary use of public transport. The employer's contribution for National Insurance is paid by the congregation.

These rates may be adjusted from time to time by the Committee in consultation with the Mission Committee and, in appropriate cases, the Mission and Service Fund may make sums available to assist congregations which cannot themselves meet these costs.

Where a Probationer serves for a full 12 month period he is entitled to one month's holiday and *pro rata* if for a shorter period.

The End of Preparation

Having, then, reached this point I am taking it that the stage of 'preparation' is at an end and I will leave it at that for the moment, returning in Chapter 4 to take up the story of progress towards ordination and becoming a fully-fledged minister.

2

Admission to the Ministry

Let it be that you are a minister of another
denomination and that for some reason you
wish to transfer to the ministry of the Church
of Scotland. Or let it be that you have been a
minister of the Church of Scotland and having
relinquished, or having been deprived of, that
status, it is your desire to enter again into the work
of the ministry within that fellowship. In either case
your way into the Kirk will have to be the Way of
Admission.

This Way of Admission forks into two branches
—it may be by Petition or it may be by Certificate
of Eligibility. In either case the procedure is in the
hands of the Committee on Probationers and
Transference and Admission of Ministers (referred to in this chapter as 'the Committee on
Admission') and its procedure is governed by the
terms of Act VIII of 1985 which bears the rather
cumbersome title, 'Anent Admission and Re-
admission of Ministers and Eligibility for Nomination, Election and Call, or for Appointment.'
These regulations superseded, but did not in terms
repeal, those of 1965. It is to be presumed that
where differences exist the later regulations will
normally prevail.

45

Admission by Petition

If a minister of any denomination other than one with which the Church of Scotland has a mutual eligibility agreement, or one in the Anglican communion, desires admission as a minister of the Church of Scotland, he must approach the General Assembly by Petition, and this involves a process which he has to initiate through the Committee on Admission. A form has to be completed setting forth various particulars, including the applicant's age, present Church connection, educational curriculum and ministerial career, as well as a statement of his reasons for wanting to enter the ministry of the Church of Scotland and of the kind of service he hopes to undertake there. He must also lodge documentary evidence in support of the information supplied, and it is usual also to submit the names of referees. The closing date for lodging a petition is 1 January preceding the Assembly to which it is addressed. At the time of lodging the petition the applicant has to pay a fee, the amount of which is determined from time to time by the Committee—at the time of writing it is £12 in the case of a minister

Interview by Committee—Synopses of petitions received are circulated to members of the Committee on Admission, which meets some time before the end of January and, unless for a very special reason he is excused, the applicant will appear then for interview. Thereafter the Committee reaches a provisional decision as to the recommendation it is going to make to the Assembly, and this is conveyed to the applicant who is required to reply in writing stating whether he wishes to proceed or to withdraw, and in the former case whether he would want in any way to alter the terms of his petition. Should he decide to withdraw he is entitled to have a proportion of anything up to one-half of his fee refunded. In exceptional cases, and for reasons to be stated in its report to the Assembly, the Committee may refer a case *simpliciter* to the Assembly.

Reference to Presbytery—The opinion of the Presbytery has now to be obtained—that is, the Presbytery of the applicant's place of residence, or if he has not resided within any one Presbytery during the past three months, the Presbytery of Edinburgh. If with permission of the Committee the applicant is already being employed within the Church (see hereunder) and has been thus for at least a month prior to 1 January, the Presbytery within whose bounds he is so employed is also to be consulted. Copies of the petition in full, of the synopsis, and of the proposed recommendation are then forwarded to the appropriate Presbytery or Presbyteries, which will consider and forward their reactions not later than 15 April.

Something of a difficulty can present itself at this stage, for the reference to the Presbytery is clearly designed to uncover any local knowledge relevant to the petitioner, particularly any reason why he should not be received, and with this in view the Presbytery would wish to give its enquiry the fullest publicity. Since, however, the Petitioner is probably in a charge of another denomination and may still withdraw his petition, it would be most unfortunate for the applicant if it were to become widely known that he was so much as contemplating leaving his denomination. The Presbytery must therefore at this stage treat the matter as confidential and deal with it behind closed doors.

Review by Committee—The Committee then meets again and reconsiders the recommendation it proposes to make—which may be (a) for granting, (b) for partially granting, (c) for deferring, or (d) for refusing to grant. The decision is intimated to the Petitioner who may alter his crave or withdraw his petition, and in the latter case all documents lodged will immediately be returned to him.

Older Applicant—In the case of an applicant over 60 years of age on 1 January in the year of his application and who has not held a charge or charges in a Presbyterian Church for at least ten years, the Committee is not to make a recommendation, although it may resolve to transmit the petition *simpliciter*. This provision, designed presumably to make the path of this kind of applicant more difficult can in my opinion have the opposite effect. The petitioner arranges for an eloquent friend to move in his favour, which he does in an impassioned *ex parte* appeal, and it is at this point that it would prove most helpful for the commissioners to have, to set alongside this, a cool, balanced, report and recommendation from the Committee, particularly if it were hostile. The Regulations prevent this.

At the Assembly—When the Petitioner is called to the bar the commissioners have in their hands copies of the petition itself and of the reports of the Committee and Presbytery or Presbyteries. The Petitioner may answer questions put from the floor or he may speak to any inaccuracy which

he claims appears in the synopsis—with a copy
of which he has been supplied at least seven
days before the hearing — but he may not speak
in support of his petition, except that he may
do so briefly in a case where the petition has
been transmitted *simpliciter* or with an adverse
recommendation.

If the Assembly resolve to grant the crave they
remit to the Presbytery concerned, or to some
other, to 'take the necessary steps'. This, as I see it,
means that on receipt of the relevant Minute of
Assembly the Presbytery adds the name of the
Petitioner to the List of Ministers Without Charge
resident within its bounds, although I think that
before doing so it should require him at least to
sign the Formula. Courtesy demands that he be
welcomed at a Presbytery meeting, but he is not
entitled to a seat in the court. If no action has been
taken on the strength of the Assembly Minute
within six months of its date of issue it loses its
validity; from which it would seem to follow that
the Petitioner acquires the status of a Minister of
the Church of Scotland not when the Assembly
grants the crave of his petition but only when the
Presbytery adds his name to its Roll. This is
perfectly reasonable. It may seem less than reasonable, though, that the Petitioner should be in
danger of losing his award because of delays which
may have been on the part of the Presbytery.

The Assembly may resolve upon partial (or
interim) admission, as will happen when it is
desired to impose conditions—for example, that
certain classes be taken (at the Petitioner's expense)
or that an assistantship be served. During such

period of interim admission the Petitioner is not to preach in a vacancy or to administer the sacraments, but he is free to exercise all the other functions of the ministry. It is not that the validity of his orders is being called into question, but that until the conditions of his acceptance have been fulfilled he is not to exercise his ordained status. He is put under the supervision of a Presbytery and within the context of discipline he will be treated as a Probationer. The following Assembly will receive a report from the Committee as to whether the Petitioner has fully and satisfactorily completed the requirements imposed, and if it is resolved to admit then procedure will be as above.

For any reason which they deem adequate, the Assembly may resolve to defer consideration of a Petition. And, of course, they may decide to refuse the crave of a Petition.

Ordained Status—If the Petitioner has been ordained to the full status of the ministry by a Presbyterian Church within the United Kingdom, by a Church overseas which is a member of the World Alliance of Reformed Churches, by any Church in the Anglican communion, or by any regularly constituted branch of the Methodist Church or of the Congregational Church (provided in the latter case the ordination was in accordance with bylaws 1959 or 1976 of the Congregational Union of Scotland), or by the United Reformed Church in the United Kingdom, then his admission will be with the status of a minister. In other cases the question of the acceptability of the Petitioner's ordination will be the subject of report by the Committee and of consideration and judgment by the Assembly. If not prepared to recognise the Petitioner's ordination the Assembly may admit him as a Licentiate and remit to a Presbytery to take the necessary steps.

Interim Employment—A prospective petitioner may apply to the Committee for permission to accept interim employment within the Church pending the outcome of his petition, and if agreeable the Committee will grant such permission subject to the restriction that he may not dispense the sacraments, that he may not preach in a vacant charge (unless a terminable appointment or a continued vacancy), and that he must report to the Clerk of the Presbytery concerned (into whose care and supervision he shall be deemed to have passed). The 'employing' Presbytery may be required to provide, within three weeks of being requested to do so, a report as to the manner in which he is performing his duties. And the permission may at any time be rescinded.

Lapsing of Admission—This part of the Act concludes with what to me appears an odd provision, in the following terms: 'In the event of a Petitioner not having received a Call to a Church, or a ministerial appointment by the fifth anniversary of his admission by the General Assembly, his admission shall be deemed to have lapsed, and, if the petitioner still seeks admission as a minister of this Church it shall be necessary for him to present a new petition to the General Assembly'.

I have three difficulties here. First, I find it strange that the Act should apply the term 'Petitioner' to a person the crave of whose petition was granted five years before and whose name during all that time has appeared on the List of a Presbytery's Ministers Without Charge. Second, I find it difficult to accept that someone on whom the status of a Minister of the Church of Scotland has been judicially conferred can be deprived of that status except as the result of a judicial process. And third, I wonder what is to be the status of such a person—obviously he will not revert to being a minister of the denomination from which he came, so it would seem he will, by the clerical act of a Committee Secretary, have been deposed from the ministry. I should think it is a situation unlikely to arise— and I should hope not!

Licentiates
A Licentiate of another denomination may petition the General Assembly craving to be received as a Licentiate of the Church of Scotland, and, with the necessary adjustments, the foregoing conditions and regulations will apply (the fee in this case being £9). If accepted, the Petitioner will be put under the care of a Presbytery which has been instructed to take 'the necessary steps'. What are the necessary steps? It is a most interesting question. It is, I think, generally accepted that there is no authority for requiring such a person to undergo trials for licence (I received this opinion from no less an authority than Dr Cox himself) and there is no power to require a Probationary Period—he has already been given the status of a Licentiate and, as soon as any conditions imposed by the Assembly have been purged, he is free to accept a call.

I must add, however, that to me it has always

seemed odd that in the case of people from a totally different tradition we should be prepared to take for granted their knowledge of the legal and sacramental practice and traditions of the Church of Scotland when we are at such pains to examine those brought up within that tradition. The General Assembly of 1946 laid it upon the Presbytery in such a case 'to satisfy itself as to the knowledge of those admitted regarding the practice and procedure of the Church as contained in the first ten chapters of *Cox*'. A knowledge of the first ten chapters of *Cox* is no mean achievement! I imagine that short of demanding trials a Presbytery is empowered to take what steps it considers reasonable in discharging this responsibility.

Students
A student who has been, or is being, trained within another denomination does not come within the province of this legislation. It is for him to apply to the Committee on Education for the Ministry which will deal with his case on its merits and the student will then enter the Kirk by the normal way of candidature.

Re-Admission by Petition

A former Minister of Licentiate of the Church of Scotland who has been deprived of, or who has voluntarily relinquished, his status, may desire re-admission, and in such a case he must submit a petition to the General Assembly. Such a petition will *mutatis mutandis* follow the same lines which apply to the case of a Petition for Admission; the

fee being £9 for a minister, £6 for a Licentiate. A
Licentiate who in terms of the new Act has allowed
himself to lose his status (*p* 49) may likewise
petition for restoration to the Roll.

Admission By Certificate of Eligibility

In certain cases, the number of which has been
steadily increasing in recent years, it is not necessary for a minister of another denomination to
petition the General Assembly asking to be received as a minister of the Church of Scotland, his
course being simply to obtain from the Committee
on Admission for a modest fee a Certificate of
Eligibility; for, when lodged with the Presbytery
Clerk through the Interim Moderator of a vacant
congregation (*p* 80), this will entitle him to be
nominated in that vacancy and thus, after election
and induction (or introduction), he will become a
minister of the Church of Scotland. Should he for
any reason be refused a Certificate of Eligibility by
the Committee such an applicant is at liberty
to approach the General Assembly by petition
craving to be received as a minister.

Requirements
The conditions that have to be satisfied to acquire a
Certificate of Eligibility vary according to the
Church from which the applicant comes—as
hereunder.
   Presbyterian Church in Ireland—To obtain a Certi-
ficate of Eligibility a minister of that Church has to
produce a certificate from the Clerk of his General
Assembly to the effect that he was ordained in that

Church and has held charges or appointments within it for a period of at least five years. The fee is £8.

Reformed Churches—A minister of any regularly constituted Presbyterian Church in the United Kingdom, of the United Reformed Church in the United Kingdom, or of any Church outwith the United Kingdom which is a member of the World Alliance of Reformed Churches, or of a Church within the Anglican communion, may obtain a Certificate of Eligibility on condition that he satisfies the Committee on Admission that he is a minister in full standing in his own denomination, that he has held charges or appointments within it for at least five years, that his educational qualifications are comparable with those required within the Church of Scotland, and that his character and conduct are becoming to his profession. The fee is £8.

Partnership Plan—A completely new conception was introduced into the 1984 Act anent Settlement of Ministers whereby a vacant congregation may decide to have as their minister for three years a minister of a Church furth of Scotland which is a member of the World Alliance of Reformed Churches, or of the Church of South India or of the Church of Pakistan. A minister chosen in this way by a Vacancy Committee must, before nomination, secure from the Committee on Admission a Certificate of Eligibility, and this will be supplied provided he can satisfy the Committee that he has fulfilled the educational requirements of, and has been ordained by, his own Church, that he is a minister in full standing, that he has served for at least three years in charges or appointments therein, and that his character and conduct are becoming to his profession.

Such a person will be introduced as minister of the vacant charge on conditions of terminable tenure for a period not exceeding three years. With concurrence of the Presbytery and of the Board of World Mission and Unity his incumbency may at the request of the congregation be extended for one further period of three years. Throughout the time of his ministry he will enjoy to the full the status of a minister of the Church of Scotland. At the end he will revert to being a minister of the Church from which he came.

Former Minister of the Church of Scotland—A former minister or licentiate of the Church of Scotland who has neither relinquished nor been deprived of his status but who falls into one of the following categories may acquire a Certificate of Eligibility on the conditions stated, the fee in each case being £4.

(1) One who with approval of the Board of World Mission and Unity has entered the courts of an indigenous Church as a full member—on ceasing to be such a member.

(2) One who has become an accredited minister of the United Reformed Church in the United Kingdom, or of the Presbyterian Church in Ireland —on production of a certificate from his Assembly Clerk as to status, record and character.

(3) One who has served furth of Scotland in a Church which is a member of the World Alliance of Reformed Churches—provided he satisfies the Committee on Admission or its Executive as to status, record and character.

(4) One who has accepted employment outwith the jurisdiction of any Church with the provision as in (3) above, and on condition that he gives a written assurance of his intention to terminate such employment.

(5) One who because of maternity commitments has not for a period been in a charge—with the provision as in (3) above.

It should be noted that in the case of ministers within categories (4) and (5) the Certificate of Eligibility is necessary for re-entry into the parish ministry, but the person concerned has in fact never lost the status of a minister of the Church of Scotland.

Conditions—All certificates issued by the Committee as above are subject to the following conditions: (a) they will not be issued in a vacuum but only in connection with a particular vacancy; (b) unless under very special circumstances, they will not be granted to persons over 60 years of age; and (c) their validity extends to only one year after the date of issue.

The End of the Way of Admission

It will be clear from the foregoing that in the case of Admission by Petition the status of minister of the Church of Scotland is conferred when the Presbytery to whose care the Petitioner has been committed takes the appropriate steps; whereas in the case of Admission by Certificate of Eligibility the status of minister of the Church of Scotland is acquired only in virtue of being inducted to a charge or installed in an appointment. Once acquired—in whichever way—the status continues to be enjoyed until relinquished, until deprivation, or until the person has entered the service of another denomination. There is one exception— in the special case of the Partnership Plan, for in that case, in my view, the person ceases to be a minister of the Church of Scotland on the termination of his service in the charge to which he was called, and this occurs whether or not he intends to return to the service of the Church from which he came.

3

The Auxiliary Ministry

The suggestion, first mooted in 1975, that the traditional full-time ministry of the Church might be supplemented by a part-time ministry took concrete shape in the Report submitted by the Committee of Forty to the Assembly of 1977. In support of the proposal two reasons, principally, were advanced: first, that as things seemed to be developing, there was never again likely to be an adequate supply of ordained personnel to man, nor an adequate flow of finance to support, a full territorial ministry of the traditional pattern throughout Scotland; and second, that 'the Church has a potential resource in terms of her lay men and women which is not being fully used'. I may be forgiven for interpolating here that to me it has always seemed strange that if we are to use laymen we must begin by ordaining them—but that is another story!

It was resolved that there should be consultation with other interested Committees and that a draft Act should be prepared for submission to the following Assembly. What actually happened in 1978 was that a further report was presented elaborating what was envisaged, and it was remitted to the General Administration Committee, in consultation with the Department of Education and the Home Board, to 'draft an Overture to enable the ordination of auxiliary part-time ministers of Word and Sacrament'. This Overture, finally approved under Barrier Act procedure (by 27 to 20) became Act IV of 1980 and contained also regulations for the selection and training of such a ministry.

Definition—An Auxiliary Minister is defined as 'a person who has been ordained for life to a ministry of Word and Sacrament exercisable under supervision on a part-time and non-stipendiary basis'. The Report of 1978 had pointed out that 'the ministry envisaged, while different in certain respects from the full-time ministry, must not be a second-rate affair .... Ordination would be to the ministry of Word and Sacrament'. No-one would wish the Auxiliary Ministry to be seen as 'second-rate', but it is quite misleading, is it not, to describe a ministry which is part-time, part-trained, unpaid, exercised only under supervision, and debarred from induction to a charge, as 'different in certain respects from the full-time ministry'. For myself I think it is both fair and accurate to think of it as a second tier of ministry. For better or for worse the long-cherished tradition of the equality of the ministry is gone. The ministry of a parish is still the highest office in the Church, but it is now being exercised at two levels. It may well be that this is for the better, but no good purpose is served by trying to pretend that we still have a single tier of ministry.

Recruitment—The recruitment of candidates is in the first instance a duty of Presbyteries, who in fulfilling it are to 'have regard to the existing and anticipated needs of the charges within their bounds'. The Report of 1978 had said specifically that 'it would be for the Presbytery, in consultation with the relevant Kirk Sessions, to identify a need for an auxiliary ministry and to seek candidates to meet that need'. This would seem to mark out a clear order of proceeding—the Presbytery should first of all have an assignment in view and should then look around for some suitable person who might be trained to undertake it. But that would scarcely make sense in respect to a need of the 'existing' variety since the course of preparation is to occupy at least three years. This situation has in experience been aggravated in a case where long-term readjustment planning had been co-ordinated with the training of an auxiliary minister, and when he decided to transfer to training for the regular ministry the whole plan fell into ruins to the discomfiture of all concerned.

It is, I think, reasonable to proceed on the basis that if a Presbytery has within its bounds a willing and likely candidate it should encourage his re-cruitment in the belief that by the time he is in a position to accept it there will be—or there will be capable of being created—a meaningful assign-ment in which he can exercise his gifts.

Recognition as a Candidate—An applicant for the auxiliary ministry must be in full communion with the Church of Scotland and must carry the recommendation of his minister and Kirk Session as well as of the Presbytery. He may be a 'she' although strangely enough in its first few years the auxiliary ministry was exclusively a masculine preserve. He must have a good educational background and 'proficiency in spoken and written English will be regarded as a matter of material importance'. He has to submit a formal application to the Committee on Education for the Ministry (referred to hereunder as 'the Committee') which will arrange for him to appear at a Selection School (*p* 21) where the standard expected in the matter of suitability is exactly as it is for the regular ministry. If satisfied with the Assessors' report the Committee accepts the applicant as a candidate in training, subject to his being nominated by his Presbytery. In view of what was said above I am taking this to mean that when it nominates a candidate the Presbytery will be guided by the Committee's assessment of his suitability and will pay no heed to its own needs—existing or anticipated.

Course of Training

The course extends over a 20 month period, is part-time, and consists of (1) central residential training, (2) extension study under both central and local tutors, and (3) practical training.

(1) This involves attendance at extended week-end training sessions held in the summer of each of the three years of the course, and it covers both academic disciplines and experience of worship.

(2) This is carried on through supervised reading and tutorial work, the written essays being submitted to the central tutors.

(3) This takes the form of a six month period each year served in a parish (not normally the candidate's own) and relates to preaching and the

conduct of public worship, to pastoral work and to Christian education.

In each year of the course the candidate must satisfy the Presbytery and the Committee of his continuing progress and suitability and, if not satisfied, the Committee has power to extend or to discontinue the course.

Although the regulations for selection and training went down as part of the Overture under the Barrier Act it is specifically provided that these may be amended on the recommendation of the Committee without being subject to Barrier Act procedure. The whole Act is in fact the subject of review by a special commitee at the time of writing.

Licence–The Committee, if the course has been completed to its satisfaction, transmits an Exit Certificate to the Presbytery, which has then to take the candidate on trials for licence (unlike the student he does not need to apply for this). The trials are exactly the same as for candidates for the full-time ministry (*p* 33), the only distinction being that the candidate is licensed not as a Preacher of the Gospel but 'to the Auxiliary Ministry of the Church of Scotland'.

Probationary Period–'The first year after licence will normally be a probationary period', although in exceptional cases exemption may be granted. The Committee is to assess the adequacy of the experience gained in light of a report from the supervising minister and, if the Committee sustains, the candidate then becomes eligible for ordination by the Presbytery. The Act says that where exemption is granted, 'ordination may follow immediately upon satisfactory completion of the course'—which seems to indicate that both licence and the trials which precede it have been by-passed. I find it hard to believe that this is intended, for I cannot conceive any reason why a person who has been excused the probationary period should for that reason be presumed to be qualified for licence. I have been interested to learn that what has in fact been happening has been that all candidates, whether or not granted exemption from the probationary period, have been required to undergo trials for licence.

Assignment

'Auxiliary Ministers may be allotted such assignments as the Presbytery of the bounds may determine', the conditions of the assignment being set forth in writing by the Presbytery after it has conferred with the minister (or Interim Moderator) and Kirk Session of the parish within which the Auxiliary is to operate. These conditions are to include a definition of the minimum amount of time to be devoted to the job by the Associate— it seems now to be generally accepted that ten hours per week is a reasonable expectation and that this should include time spent in preparation. The conditions are also to include provisions regarding payment of pulpit supply fees and reimbursement of expenses incurred. It is laid down that the duration of an assignment is not to exceed five years and therefore, presumably, that the length of the assignment is to be stated in the written paper of conditions.

Review–The Act says (Section 15), 'The Presbytery of the bounds shall be entitled at any time to carry out a review of any assignment, and, in the light of such review (a) to suspend or terminate the assignment, (b) ... to renew the assignment for a further period not exceeding five years, (c) ... to vary the conditions regulating the assignment'. This makes strange reading. These conditions of assignment, solemnly set forth in writing, have all the appearance of a contract of service and I find it hard to believe that one party to that contract is to be at liberty to vary the conditions and even to terminate the engagement on its own simple say-so. If, as would appear to be the case, the Auxiliary is bound by the written conditions, he is surely entitled at the very least to be consulted and his consent secured before alterations can be effected.

In 1985 on the Report of the Maintenance of the Ministry Committee there were submitted proposals entitled 'Proposed Conditions for the Assignment of an Auxiliary Minister' and these were duly approved although they were not incorporated into the Act, nor was the Act amended. These proposals deal with the foregoing criticisms to the extent of declaring that the second paragraph of any agreement is to state 'that the assignment is to be for five years in the first instance but is subject to review at any time at the request of the minister (or Interim Moderator) and Kirk Session, the Auxiliary Minister, or the Presbytery'; and the eighth paragraph is to declare 'the conditions under which alterations may be made in the conditions of assignment'. Apart from the fact that five years is maximum and not mandatory, this seems a vast improvement. But the

Act is still there, and in law it is the Act that prevails.

Pulpit Supply Fees–The Act also lays down (Section 11) that the written conditions 'shall further include provisions regarding payment of pulpit supply fees'. I understand from the Secretaries of the Maintenance of the Ministry Committee that not at any time have fees in respect of pulpit supply given in the pulpit of his assignment been paid to an Auxiliary. If what the Act means is that fees are not to be paid, it would be difficult to conceive a more confusing or ineffective way of saying it: if the Act means what it seems to say, then in each case there should be room for discussion as to what is to happen in respect of fees, and the 1985 Maintenance of the Ministry report referred to is in contravention of the Act. For it spells out the matter with great clarity, providing that the agreement is to make plain, 'that the auxiliary minister shall not receive any pulpit supply fee for any service conducted in connection with the assignment, nor shall he or she be permitted to conduct services or administer the sacraments during a vacancy in the charge other than those required normally in connection with the assignment'. The Auxiliary may, however, with permission of the supervising minister, accept engagements elsewhere and receive payment in respect of these. This has the great advantage that it is clear—but whether it strictly construes the Act is another question.

Relation to Courts–Throughout the period of the assignment the Auxiliary is to be associated with a Kirk Session which will normally be that of the parish where he is working, and he may act as its Moderator *pro tempore*—strictly on the terms that apply to such a Moderator. He will not be a member of Session and will have no vote. Also during the period of the assignment he is a full member of the Presbytery and also of the Synod and is eligible to receive a commission to the General Assembly.

Under Supervision—'In discharging the duties of his assignment an auxiliary minister shall be subject to the oversight of a minister or ministers appointed by the Presbytery of the bounds.' It is to be presumed that such a minister will be in fact the minister of the parish, for otherwise problems could arise in regard to intrusion.

Conditions of Assignment

According to the Maintenance of the Ministry report of 1985 the written conditions of assignment should extend to at least nine paragraphs, with the possibility of additional ones 'as may seem good to the Presbytery'. They are as follows:

(1) Fixes a date for ordination (if appropriate) and for the beginning of the assignment, and defines the physical area of the assignment.

(2) States the length of the assignment (maximum of five years) and the conditions under which that length may be reviewed.

(3) Indicates clearly to whom the auxiliary is responsible in the fulfilment of his ministry, and defines any special duties and responsibilities he has to undertake.

(4) Declares the minimum number of hours per

week and the number of weeks per annum which the auxiliary is to devote to the work.

(5) Sets forth in detail the arrangements for, and the rates of reimbursement of, outlays—travelling at the usual rates of up to a maximum of 4500 miles per annum, telephone calls (not rental), and so on.

(6) Deals with payment of pulpit supply fees (see above).

(7) Outlines arrangements for the Presbytery to receive reports on the working of the assignment annually, or as may be required.

(8) Indicates the conditions under which alterations may be made in the conditions of the assignment (see above).

(9) States with which Kirk Session the Auxiliary is to be associated and declares that he may preside thereat, but only in the capacity of Moderator *pro tempore*. (As a minister he may preside over any Kirk Session in this capacity.)

Ordination

On the completion of, or on being granted exemption from, the period of probation, the Licentiate for the Auxiliary Ministry may be ordained by his Presbytery, although one would expect that this would normally follow upon his being allotted an assignment. Since the service he is to render is part-time it is to be expected that the assignment will be fairly near his place of residence. It may take a variety of forms and may even, I imagine, consist of a kind of roving commission within the Presbytery, or at least within some limited part of it. He cannot be inducted to a parish, but his assignment may consist in ministering to a parish, and it would be reasonable for him to begin his duties with some sort of Service of Introduction. It would seem fitting that in the case of his first assignment this should be coupled with the Service of Ordination. The Act makes no reference to the matter but I take the view that an edict in common form should be served either in his own church or in the church connected with the assignment, as would be done in the case of either minister or elder. The Service would follow the identical pattern to that for the ordination of a probationer for the work of an ordained assistantship.

The End of the Way

Having been duly ordained the aspirant to the Auxiliary Ministry has now gained the status of a minister of the Church of Scotland. So far as status is concerned he is in the fullest and most complete sense a minister. Section 2 of the Act declares, 'Except in so far as modified by the terms of this Act an auxiliary minister is declared to be a minister of the Church of Scotland for all necessary purposes in connection with his or her assignment as hereunder provided'. What this seems to say is that within the limits set for the exercise of his ministry that ministry is perfect and complete in every way.

In all matters of discipline the Auxiliary is answerable to the Presbytery. His status continues for life unless he is judicially deprived of it or voluntarily relinquishes it, but his membership of the courts depends upon his fulfilling an assignment and terminates with the end of that assignment. When not 'employed' as a minister he can still be associated with a Kirk Session, but he cannot sit in the courts of the Church as an elder.

4

Securing Appointment to a Parish

The opening chapter followed the course of the aspirant to the ministry through the process of selection, the course of study, and the service of probationary period, right up to that point where he becomes eligible to receive a call to a parish or to take on any one of a variety of appointments available within the Church. In the present chapter it will be my aim to indicate the steps that have to be taken on the remaining stage of the journey towards becoming the ordained minister of a parish. As indicated above, he may of course be ordained for some other form of ministry, and these are dealt with elsewhere. The parish ministry is still, however, the standard pattern, and the entry to that ministry is a complicated affair governed by the terms of the Act anent Settlement of Ministers (Act IV of 1984), In the case of probationers, certain additional conditions are imposed under the Act of 1985 anent Students *etc*, so let us begin by getting these cleared out of the way.

Preaching in Vacancies

In December of each year the Committee on Education for the Ministry supplies the Committee

71

on Probationers with a list of names of those whose Probationary Period seems likely to be sustained, and the latter body from January onwards includes the names of a selection of these people when sending lists to Vacancy Committees. The Probationer is himself at perfect liberty at this point himself to apply for a vacancy, but in that case the Vacancy Committee is required to obtain written permission from the Probationers Committee before he may be put forward as a nominee to be heard by the congregation. And although a probationer may in fact be elected to a vacant charge while still serving his probationary period, this must have been completed to the satisfaction of all concerned before he can be inducted to the charge.

Keeping Name on Roll—If by the second anniversary of his being licensed a person has not secured an appointment involving ordination, he is required to complete a fresh form for the Probationers' Committee outlining his up-to-date position. If within one year thereafter he has not provided this information, his name is to be taken from the Roll; a like fate is to overtake any licentiate of three years' standing whose whereabouts are not known to the Committee. Once a name has been removed in this way it may be restored only by application for a Certificate of Eligibility or by petition to the General Assembly. That is to say, failure to keep the Committee informed will not endanger status, but it will involve the person concerned in considerable inconvenience before his name reappears on the List.

First Charge Restriction

Since we are dealing here with preliminary hurdles, this may be a convenient point at which to say a word concerning the restriction laid on a minister in his first charge—that he should stay there for at least five years. It was in 1959 that legislation was introduced requiring this. The thinking behind the Act was something like this. The third year of a man's ministry can be a highly critical period—the first enthusiasm has waned (on both sides), the impetus of the new beginning is spent, things are not going nearly as well as had been expected, dreams are unfulfilled, hopes unrealised. And it is so easy to blame it all on the charge and imagine the answer lies in fresh woods and pastures new. At such a time a man may need to be protected from himself. Let him run away and he may well go on repeating that pattern and become what the late Principal Macgregor described as 'an itinerant catastrophe'. Let him stay to get his second wind and he may stay for many a long year and have a most fruitful and happy ministry. There may, of course, be unusual circumstances which would justify an exception being made, and the Act allows for this, but it has to be testified *before nomination* in the name of the releasing Presbytery, either in a Minute of Presbytery or in a Certificate subscribed by Moderator, Clerk and two other members of Presbytery.

One or two points are worthy of attention in this connection. First, that it applies only to a first charge. Second, that it is not directed against 'young ministers'—it applies to a first charge and has nothing to do with the age of the person

concerned. Third, that it is a 'charge of a Church
and Parish of the Church of Scotland' and therefore although a man may have spent some years as,
say, a Chaplain to the Forces or in a charge
of another denomination, neither of these is a
'charge' within the meaning of this Act. Fourth,
that the five year period is to be calculated from
the date of induction to the date of nomination,
not to the date when he might be expected to be
inducted to the new charge—although I imagine
no great fuss would be made about a month or two.
And last, and very important, that if recourse is to
be had to the 'exceptional circumstances' clause the
appropriate certificate must be secured *prior to
nomination*—once there has been the publicity
attending nomination, the releasing Presbytery will
find itself more or less blackmailed into granting
the certificate.

The Vacant Charge

What follows is primarily directed at the case of a
probationer seeking his first charge, but it is
equally applicable to the minister who, already in a
charge, is seeking a change of scene. Indeed any
minister who has spent at least five years in his
present charge and who is desirous of a move
should intimate accordingly to the Committee on
Probationers and Transference and Admission of
Ministers who will find opportunities for him to be
heard in vacancies.

In Search of a Minister—At any moment of time
there are a number of charges vacant (probably
just over 100 all told), and of these a proportion

are not merely vacant but are actively engaged looking for a minister. That is to say, they have successfully passed the readjustment test, having been given permission to call by the Presbytery with concurrence of the Assembly's Unions and Readjustments Committee; they have their Electoral Register prepared and their Vacancy Committee appointed; and the latter is busily engaged in the search for some person or persons to nominate to the congregation—most likely for one person to be a sole nominee, but possibly for a number of persons to constitute a leet. It may be a simple straightforward case of a single charge of the traditional pattern in town or in country; or perhaps it is a linked charge; or it may be a case of deferred union or deferred linking where the minister elected is to begin as minister of A and later to become minister of AB or of A linked with B; it may be a case where the choice is restricted, perhaps to a probationer, perhaps to a minister not under the age of, say, 55; or it may be a case of terminable tenure where although the minister will be inducted he will have no security of tenure beyond the guarantee of at least six months' written notice that his incumbency is to end.

Once you reach the stage of being interested in filling a particular vacancy you will be very well advised to discover at an early stage exactly what is the position—especially if it is a case of terminable tenure. In such circumstances there will be available somewhere a Minute setting forth the terms governing the appointment. The Interim Moderator will be able to supply you with a copy of this and you will be wise to study its terms with care, seeking advice if these terms are not clear to you.

List of Vacant Charges—The Department of Ministry and Mission is under obligation to maintain an up-to-date monthly list of all vacant charges looking for ministers, and this, if not already supplied, may be obtained on application. In the case of probationers it is supplied as a matter of course beginning in the January preceding completion of the probationary period.

'Applications are Invited'—Vacant congregations incline more and more to advertising in the press and when they do they will normally 'invite applications'. Not all congregations do this, and indeed some are bitterly hostile to the whole conception of advertisement and application in the conviction that this is an attempt to interfere with the free working of the Holy Spirit. By the same token there are ministers and probationers who would never agree to submit an application, and that on conscientious grounds. One must respect such views when honestly held, although for my own part I find it hard to believe that any divine plan is capable of being so easily frustrated at our puny hands, and I certainly think that submitting an application is characterised by an honesty lacking from—as the custom of a few is—the arrangement that some second party will put forward my name and press my claims.

If an application is to be submitted it is a document worthy of being treated with considerable care. A very sound idea is to put it to the test of reading it over and saying, 'Now, if I were a member of a Vacancy Committee and had this put into my hand what kind of picture would I be likely to form of the writer?' An application can tell the discriminating reader a great deal (a) by what is actually written, (b) by the way in which it is all set forth, (c) by the general tone and character of the writing, and (d) by what it does not say. Manufacturers spend a lot of money employing the best brains to set out their products in a telling way. You just cannot afford to present yourself carelessly in any application you submit. Of course you are not wanting to 'blow your own horn', but this is a case where you have to play your own horn and you are better to play it up to a high standard of musical excellence.

Being Heard—Vacancy Committees, I am afraid, do not always operate on the most business-like lines, so that while you may well receive an acknowledgment of the application upon which you have lavished so much time and thought, the chances are that you may not. It may well be that after many weeks you may hear from them that they are interested in your candidature and wish to pursue the matter. Alternately you may hear after some months that they are grateful for your interest but that someone else has been chosen. And quite literally you may never hear from them at all. Not hearing anything about the fate of your application does not necessarily mean that it has found its way into some wastepaper basket—the Committee may, unbeknown to you, have sent a scouting party to hear you. In the case of the placed minister this is generally fairly easy (although it is surprising how often they arrive when a stranger is in the pulpit), but in the case of the

probationer the situation is not so straightforward
and the chances are they will have to write asking
you to make yourself 'audible'. Similarly if you—or
they—are in a remote area, a fair amount of
organisation may be involved and considerable
out-of-pocket expenditure incurred. They should
ask for a note of such outlays, but even if they do
not, it should be submitted.

Nomination—Ultimately the Vacancy Committee
have to abandon their Sunday outings and come to
grips with the problem of settling on a nominee.
By this time the philandering stage is past and we
are thinking seriously of marriage. That is a two-
way contract, and by this time both sides have got
to take the business very seriously—you no less
than they. In my view you should not allow
yourself to become a sole nominee unless your
attitude is that if elected you will be prepared to
accept. If after having been nominated you withdraw then not only the Vacancy Committee but the
whole congregation are put in a most invidious
situation, for the facts having by this time achieved
considerable publicity it is no longer possible to
approach the second choice who would have been
completely acceptable and probably delighted to
go.

Full Information—Since, then, you are in effect
committing yourself, you are entitled to the fullest
information regarding the charge. A heart-to-
heart talk with the Interim Moderator can be an
excellent starting-off point. It may be that a sense
of loyalty to the vacant charge will prevent his
speaking too freely, but here, as with the application, what is not said can be to the discerning ear

more significant than what is. A meeting too with the Vacancy Committee can be most helpful—from both sides. Indeed the chances are that they will ask for this. You should also have a chance to see all the 'plant', including, of course, the manse and the manse grounds. Any serious reservations in regard to any of these matters should be freely expressed and discussed and firm assurances rather than airy promises secured on salient points. In the case of a former United Presbyterian congregation operating under its original constitution, the law requires that a copy of the current constitution is to be put in your hand at this stage. If you have a serious notion that you wish to live in your own house rather than in the manse then, as I see it, this is the time at least to broach the subject. It is important that all this should be dealt with at the point when you accept nomination, not left until the Sunday when you preach as sole nominee.

Leet—As has been said, nomination may be 'sole' or as one of a leet. The latter is today very unusual, but it is still a possibility. At the time when the 1984 legislation on vacancies was being framed, Presbyteries were asked for their views on the question of whether sole nomination might perhaps be made the only method of proceeding. To this question, 28 Presbyteries said 'Yes', 9 said 'No', the others standing somewhere in between. The general position of the No stance was, '*We* don't like it, but we don't think *they* should be deprived of a right of such long standing'. Accordingly the option was continued, but only in the belief that it would ultimately go through desuetude, and that it was better it should go that way.

Should you find yourself presented with an invitation to preach as one of a leet, you should give the matter very careful thought. In doing so you should bear in mind that when a leet is chosen, the Presbytery Advisory Committee is entitled to add further names up to the number chosen by the Vacancy Committee and that these too have to be heard and voted upon by the congregation. Unless you are extraordinarily keen on the charge it's not a choice to be recommended.

Letter of Acceptance

If you have decided to accept nomination then you should write to the Secretary of the Vacancy Committee intimating accordingly, and with your letter you should enclose, if this is not already in the hands of the Interim Moderator, (a) if you are a Probationer, a Certificate from the Education for the Ministry Committee to the effect that you have satisfactorily completed, or have been exempted from, the Probationary Period, (b) if you have not completed five years in your present charge, being your first charge, the relevant Certificate from your present Presbytery, (c) if you have been admitted to the Church of Scotland on petition an extract Minute of Assembly to that effect, (d) in other appropriate cases a Certificate of Eligibility, or (e) when the charge is 'Gaelic essential' a certificate of competence to preach in Gaelic. I must confess I do not know how or where this is obtained.

Preaching as Nominee—Arrangements will then be made for you to preach as nominee and also in

connection with the subsequent election. Usually at
this stage the Kirk Session is desperate to get
everything achieved at great speed although—or
perhaps because—many weeks may have been
wasted in the earlier stages. It is important to resist
the rush and to choose a date that is suitable in
every way and which, as far as possible, will gear in
neatly with the dates of Presbytery meetings. All
expenses incurred in connection with such preaching, including the cost of supplying your own
pulpit when this is involved, are to be met by the
vacant congregation.

Withdrawal—It is in order at any time between
nomination and election to withdraw. Indeed you
may withdraw right up to the actual moment of
induction—and people have done so. Obviously
this is a very serious step which will greatly
incommode the vacant congregation, but if facts
emerge which convince the nominee that it would
be a mistake for him to proceed the better course
for him is to take the situation in hand and draw
out. The same is true even after election, and if the
election is a divided one showing substantial
opposition, or revealing perhaps that there is deep
division within the congregation, or if as the result
of his visit the nominee gets a completely new and
unhappy impression of the whole set-up, then the
wise course may be for him to get out. Surely not
a step to be taken lightly, but in certain circumstances the lesser of two evils.

Letter Giving the Usual Assurances—If you are
prepared to accept election then you should
without delay write, this time to the Interim
Moderator, to this effect, and you should include

in your letter an assurance that you have used no undue influence either by yourself or by others to secure the appointment. This is generally referred to as 'a letter giving the usual assurances'. The background to this is not without interest.

In 1888 an Act was passed to bring the legislation against Simoniacal Practices into line with the new system of ministerial election that had emerged consequent on the abolition of patronage four years earlier. The story from the Book of Acts, chapter 8, will be remembered of how Simon the Sorcerer wished to purchase the gift of the Holy Spirit with money. The legislation had been directed against what under patronage was a quite real danger—that a minister might enter into a bargain with a patron that if he became minister of the charge he would not at any time seek for an augmentation of stipend, for improvements to the manse, for an enlargement of the Church building, or whatever—that he could in effect 'buy' the living. It was ordained in the 1888 Act that the whole text of the Act (a page and a half of it) was to be read at every act of admission. Not surprisingly perhaps this in 1903 was changed to the effect that in place of the reading it would suffice if the candidate gave written assurance 'that the Act XVII of 1888 is known to me and that I have done nothing at variance with it'. Normal practice today is that in accepting appointment by letter the appointee gives 'the usual assurances'—which emphatically do not include an assurance that he has read the relevant Act or indeed that he knows of its existence! The standard form of words is as indicated—that he has used no undue influence by himself or others to secure the call.

The Call

Every time an election has been concluded it is immediately followed by the preparation of a Call addressed to the person elected. If the election has been by open vote, arrangements are usually made for the Call to be available for signature immediately thereafter, but when the election has been by ballot the signing must await the declaration of the result. In either case it must lie for at least eight days, and it must simply 'lie'—to canvass it is illegal. A name may, however, be added by mandate in the case of someone unable for any reason to attend where the Call is 'lying'. It then goes to the Presbytery to be considered along with the other papers in connection with the election. If the person called is a probationer it is usual, although not obligatory, for him to appear at the Presbytery when the election is dealt with, and if he is so present the Moderator will, when intimating the judgment of the Presbytery, place the Call in his hand. If he is in a charge the Call will be sent with the other papers to the releasing Presbytery.

The Call is of very ancient origin and in the days of patronage it represented the only response which the members could make to the appointment of their minister who had been chosen for them by the chief heritor. It was a concurrence on their part in a choice which had been none of their making. In the years of conflict leading up to the Disruption the Call came to acquire a much magnified significance, culminating in 1834 in the passing of the Veto Act. This Act laid down that 'it shall be an instruction to Presbyteries that if, at the moderating of a call to a vacant pastoral charge, the major part of the male heads of families, members of the vacant congregation, and in full communion with the Church, shall disapprove of the person in whose favour the call is proposed, such disapproval shall be sufficient ground for the Presbytery rejecting such person'. That is to say, the Presbytery was not merely empowered, it was obliged, to reject any person to whom more than half of the heads of families objected—the Presbytery was not to consider the nature or the value of the objections, merely to count the heads of the objectors. This was reasonable enough on the ground that acceptability to the congregation was a most important factor to be considered in the case of any proposed settlement—far more important, it was argued, than a knowledge of Hebrew or history or theology, on all of which he was so assiduously tested. It has to be recognised that feeling was running so high that it was enough that a minister was the nominee of the patron for him to be unacceptable. The fact that the Presbytery obeyed this injunction in the case of a presentation to the Parish of Auchterarder led to the famous case of that name, a case that went twice to the House of Lords and which ultimately, probably more than any other single factor, made the Disruption an inevitability.

Within the Free Church the call took on a new significance. Full of zeal in their new-found freedom of choice, congregations tended to set up long leets and to stage preaching competitions. In such circumstances the Call is very important, for I might have voted for Mr B, but it was Mr E who topped the poll. The Call provided me with an opportunity of declaring that although another would have been my choice Mr E could count on my whole-hearted loyalty and support.

The Call is still a most important element in the settlement of a minister and a candidate would still be entitled to turn down an election on the ground that the Call was too poorly signed to justify his coming. On the other hand, of course, he might take the view that if the spiritual life of the congregation was at so low an ebb that people would not lift a pen to sign a Call, it was high time he was there to get things stirring!

Admission

All that now remains is for the person elected to be inducted to the charge. The first step, though, is for the Presbytery to sustain the election and call, and, if the person called is already in a charge, for his own Presbytery to agree to his translation. It means too that if the person called is a probationer the service will be one of ordination and induction.

Ordination—The Church of Scotland has never entertained a particularly 'high' view of ordination, defining it simply as 'the solemn setting apart of a person to some public Church office'. In the case of a minister the office has been seen as the ministry of Word and Sacrament. In early days both Word and Sacrament were believed to belong wholly to the ordained minister, but recent years have witnessed a complete change of attitude in respect of the ministry of the Word. At no time has there been any relaxation of the doctrine that the dispensation of the Sacraments belongs exclusively to the minister; and that is also the contemporary

situation, although a recent report from the Panel
on Doctrine on the subject of 'Ministry' might seem
to cast doubt on this. How far the present position
is based on theological considerations and how far
it is designed for the maintenance of good order is
an interesting question to which I do not propose
to offer an answer. For my present purpose it is
sufficient to say that this is the position.

The right to wear 'bands' follows upon ordination.

Translation–When a call is addressed to a minister in a charge, whether in the same Presbytery or
in another, the move envisaged is called 'translation', and the consent of the Presbytery is required.
The Clerk will issue an edict (one Sunday's reading
suffices) calling a meeting of the congregation at
the close of service the following Sunday when
they will consider their interest in the call addressed
to their minister and appoint representatives to
attend the meeting of Presbytery when the matter
is to be discussed. Who should preside at this
meeting? If it were possible without undue inconvenience for the prospective Interim Moderator to
do so (either by exchange of pulpit or by hurrying
over after his own service), this is the perfect
answer; otherwise the Session Clerk may preside.
It is certainly undesirable, constitutional though it
may be, that the minister himself should do so.
Time was, particularly in congregations of the
Secessions, when the translation of a minister
might be hotly contested (we read of one case
where it is said that the Presbytery spent eight
hours debating the issue); in my own time I have
never known of such a case—the congregation
always concur, and are generally gracious enough
to add that they do so reluctantly.

Confidentiality—A question sometimes asked in the case of a minister receiving a call concerns when he should disclose the fact to his present congregation. There is no law on the subject, but my own impression is that as soon as he has accepted nomination in a vacancy, a minister should call together the members of his Kirk Session and inform them, and that he should intimate officially from the pulpit on the first Sunday thereafter. To make a disclosure earlier than this is strictly a breach of confidentiality, to delay longer is to run a grave risk of the news being 'leaked'—which is always unfortunate. And telling his congregation that he has accepted nomination does not commit him irrevocably to going.

The Service—The Presbytery meets *in hunc effectum* and functions as a court on the occasion of the induction of a minister to a charge, whether or not ordination is involved. The proceedings begin with a short act of worship, after which the Clerk reads a brief narrative of proceedings leading up to the occasion. The Moderator reads the Preamble and puts the prescribed questions; the inductee having answered these signs the Formula, and the Moderator leads in prayer with all the ministerial brethren joining in the physical act of the laying on of hands in the case of an ordination. The person is then declared to be inducted and the right hand of fellowship is extended by all members of Presbytery present. A question is then put to the congregation after which charges are given to the new minister and to the congregation by a minister appointed for the purpose. After service the Presbytery resumes its session when the new minister's name is added to the Roll of Presbytery and the Interim Moderator is thanked and discharged. A certified intimation of induction is given by the Presbytery Clerk to the Session Clerk to be engrossed in the Minute of the next Session meeting, and a certified extract of the stipend arrangements is given by the Presbytery Clerk to the new minister.

Linked Charge–Where induction is to a linked charge the Presbytery has to decide in which of the Churches the service is to take place, and if the geographical situation is such that there are genuine difficulties preventing the members of the other congregation or congregations from attending, then a Service of Introduction may at a later time be held in one of these Churches. There will, however, be only one Service of Induction because, this being admission to a charge and not to a congregation, the service has the effect of admitting the inductee as minister of both or of all the congregations which go to form the one linked charge. Likewise as with the case of Deferred Union or Deferred Linking, the minister will be inducted in the Church vacant at the time, but he will be inducted by anticipation to the united or linked charge and when the time comes for the readjustment to be effective, there will be held a Service of Union (Linking) and of Introduction of Mr AB as Minister of the United (Linked) Charge.

Right Hand of Fellowship–The giving of the right hand of fellowship may seem something of a sociable formality but in fact this is not so. As Mair puts it—'Admission is a judicial act of Presbytery. The law expressly connects giving the hand with admission ... It is the completion, the overt sign, of the judicial act of admission'. The fact that this should be so confirms my conviction that a tendency I have observed, when the inductee happens to be a lady, of supplementing the right hand with a kiss on the cheek, is an unauthorised innovation to be strenuously discouraged.

Position of Associates—It is usual today that the neighbouring ministers of other denominations are invited to attend the ordination and/or induction service and are officially welcomed by the Moderator and invited to be associated with the Presbytery. A question is sometimes raised regarding the part which such visitors should take in the actual act of ordination and admission. My own view of the legal position—for what it is worth—is that all ministers of any denomination whose orders are acceptable to the Church of Scotland can properly take part in the laying on of hands, but that, for reasons discussed in the preceding paragraph, only members of the Presbytery, ministers and elders, should join in giving the right hand of fellowship. I appreciate that this could lead to all kinds of practical difficulties, and each Presbytery must be the judge of how it wishes to proceed, but the foregoing I believe to be the constitutional position.

Robes—Another practical question. It is, I think, invariable practice for all ministerial members of Presbytery to robe for such a service. Should the inductee also wear pulpit robes? In my opinion, no. It seems to me very fitting that he should wear a cassock and, if already ordained, bands. These are, if you will, symbols of his status. But robes, it seems to me, are symbols that the status is being exercised—and that certainly does not apply in the case of the inductee.

Ad Vitam aut Culpam

In olden days induction to a charge was invariably *ad vitam aut culpam* (till death or serious fault)—a system that conferred great security, even if it did so at the expense of considerable rigidity. Like so much else in this realm it dated from the days of patronage and represented the essential strength of the Kirk under that bondage, for it meant that while the patron had the right to present whom he would, his authority ended abruptly at that point and the minister once inducted was complete master of the situation—under authority, needless to add, of the Presbytery.

In those far-off days the term invariably used was 'admission' and it was comparable with infeftment (the entering into possession of land by the symbolic use of sasines), and as a consequence of it the minister took 'actual, real, and corporate possession' of 'parsonage and vicarage teinds, manse, glebe, and kirklands'. Since 1843 the word in most common use is 'induction' and all the security it nowadays confers is whatever tenure it has been agreed the inductee is to enjoy.

It is only within the past 25 years that steps have been taken to whittle away the security which a minister enjoyed in his living, but during that period the changes effected have been considerable—as briefly narrated hereunder.

In 1960 power was given in the Act anent

Congregations in an Unsatisfactory State whereby Presbyteries could in certain circumstances and without having to prove *culpa*, dissolve the pastoral tie and declare the charge vacant.

In 1972 legislation was passed providing that a minister attaining his seventieth birthday (while not culpable!) was to have the same effect, 'as if he had resigned his charge and such date had been appointed by the Presbytery of the bounds' for his demission. This applies to all ministers inducted since the passing of the Act (May 1972), except that one inducted to a charge before that date and whose charge has subsequently become a new charge in consequence of readjustment is deemed to have a right *ad vitam aut culpam* in that new charge (Act IV 1974).

In 1974 the Assembly agreed that for purposes of National Insurance ministers should be regarded as 'employed persons not contracted out' in terms of the 1975 Social Security Act—which clearly puts the minister in a relationship to the Church in respect of his living which is vastly different from that of his eighteenth century predecessor.

In 1984 the Act anent Congregations in Changed Circumstances was passed, conferring on Presbyteries in certain circumstances the right to 'terminate a minister's tenure of his charge'— although it protected all existing rights.

Also in 1984, the Readjustment Act provided that a minister might be inducted to a charge under conditions of 'terminable tenure', which means that the incumbency is deliberately designed to be terminable at the will of the Presbytery. In my view—which may not be universally shared—it might in exceptional cases be for a specific period, three or five years perhaps. More likely it will be terminable simply at the will of the Presbytery on giving six months' notice in writing; and a Minute to this effect is to be put into the hands of the candidate and his acceptance of the terms in writing received at the time of his appointment.

From all of which it must be clear that, as I stated above, induction today confers security within very strict limits—but within these limits it is a quite real security and puts the incumbent clear of the whim no less of the Church courts than of the members of his congregation.

Vacancy Schedule (Maintenance of the Ministry)— Immediately permission to call is granted a Vacancy Schedule is sent by the Maintenance of the Ministry Committee to the Treasurer of the vacant congregation, and this, after completion, has to be approved by the Presbytery and by the Assembly's Committee. In a case of linking, it is in fact a separate schedule that is issued in respect of each of the constituent congregations, although they add together to form one basis of stipend. The schedule sets forth in detail the financial arrangements regarding stipend and the sources from which it will come, the aid that will be given to or received from the Minimum Stipend Fund, and the ministerial expenses that will be met. Its general terms will, presumably, have been discussed with the candidate at some time before he accepted nomination, but by that stage it was no longer a subject for bargaining on his part. The Vacancy Committee could not, even if they wanted to, say, 'We'll add another £500 to the stipend if you'll agree to come'. For better or worse the stipend arrangements are fixed for the incumbency, although they may later be altered by means of a Revision Schedule.

On the day of his induction the minister is given by the Presbytery Clerk an extract Minute of the Assembly Committee setting forth the terms of the Vacancy Schedule. This does not form the basis of a legal contract—the minister could not sue for stipend if the full sum indicated were not being paid—rather it represents the honest intention of all concerned, and every effort will be made to ensure that its terms are honoured to the full.

Appointments in Shetland

The General Assembly of 1986 approved special regulations to apply in the Presbytery of Shetland for appointment to charges therein. When after the occurrence of a vacancy it is agreed that a further ministerial appointment is necessary, a Committee (consisting of Conveners and Secretaries from the Maintenance of the Ministry and Unions and Readjustments Commitees with the Presbytery Clerk and two elders chosen by the Presbytery) is to nominate four representatives who, together with the Presbytery Clerk and a congregational representative, are to bring forward a nomination 'for the Committee to appoint to the vacant charge'. The person so chosen is to preach in the vacant pulpit and the congregation is to have the right to reject, in which case a further nomination will be made. A minister so appointed has to undertake to serve for five years in the first instance with an option at the end of the period to indicate if he wishes to continue an appointment in Shetland for a further agreed period.

A report on the working of this scheme is to be given to the Assembly by the Committee in 1991.

Appointment to Church Extension Charge

The responsibility for appointing a minister to a Church Extension charge lies with the Assembly's Church Extension Committee in consultation with the Presbytery, and is governed by a series of Regulations (1955,1; 1969,9; 1975,2).

No Congregation—When the charge has only recently been planted and there is still no congregation, the Committee makes a choice of a minister or licentiate and invites the concurrence of the Presbytery. The Presbytery, if it agrees with the nomination, has now to go on and take steps, along normal lines as far as possible, towards a settlement. The Service of Induction will usually be held in a neighbouring Church and the edict will be served in that same Church—although if Church property is in the process of being erected, a copy of the edict might be displayed on a board at the site. The Presbytery will also have appointed a Provisional Kirk Session consisting of Assessor Elders from neighbouring charges to work with the new minister in the pioneering situation that is involved. Such cases are rare today, although they were common enough during the days of the urban sprawl.

Existing Congregation—Until it is granted full status on petition to the General Assembly, a

Church Extension charge does not enjoy the right to choose and call a minister in the usual way. On a vacancy occurring, the initiative lies with the Presbytery which consults with the Assembly's Committee regarding an appointment. The latter body then tenders a suggestion, and if this is acceptable to the Presbytery, the Interim Moderator arranges for the nominee to preach in the vacant pulpit, after which he (the Moderator) is to 'learn the mind' of the congregation, and the result of his 'learning' is then to be transmitted to the Assembly Committee. If dissatisfaction has been expressed, a second nomination will be made, and a third; but after that the Assembly Committee will proceed to make an appointment with concurrence of the Presbytery. Once an acceptable candidate has been found, it is for the Presbytery to proceed in a fashion as nearly normal as circumstances will permit, including provision for the congregation to sign a Call—after all, the right of call was for a long time exercised in circumstances highly comparable to these. The Regulations give no hint of how the mind of the congregation is to be 'learnt' by the Interim Moderator, but I imagine this would be done best by holding a meeting after the nominee has preached and then inviting reactions. The main thing is, presumably, to avoid giving the impression that this is an election—it is more nearly akin to the exercise of a power of veto.

Status—A minister appointed in either of the above ways has full ministerial standing in the Presbytery and, with his provisional Kirk Session, is responsible in the usual way for the area allotted to the charge as its provisional parish.

Appointment to a Church for the Deaf

A minister may now be ordained specifically and exclusively for work among the deaf, the procedure being governed by Assembly Acts of 1969 and 1973. The local Society for the Deaf is to approach the Presbytery of the bounds within which their Church is situated asking for the ordination of a candidate and showing (a) that he is a member in full communion with the Church of Scotland, (b) that he holds a diploma of the Deaf Welfare Examination Board, (c) that he has attended classes in a Divinity Faculty, taking classes satisfactorily in Divinity and Scottish Church History, and (d) that he has served with acceptance for at least five years in a Society for the Deaf. The Assembly Mission Committee is then to confer with the Presbytery and the Education for the Ministry Committee as to whether further training is required. A petition may then be presented to the Assembly and if granted it only remains for the Presbytery to take the candidate on trials for licence, after which he may be ordained—but exclusively for work among the deaf, a restriction which may be removed only by the General Assembly.

Alternately, any minister or licentiate of the Church of Scotland, provided he holds the appropriate diploma for work among the deaf, may be invited to become minister of a Church for the Deaf, and if he accepts he will be introduced by the Presbytery on the basis of a tenure which may be terminated by the Society for the Deaf, but only with the concurrence of the Presbytery.

In either case the minister so appointed once introduced has full ministerial status and enjoys a seat in Presbytery and Synod.

5

Duties of a Parish Minister

While the object of this chapter will be to define the various duties of a minister in a parish, opportunity will be taken to comment in passing on rights and privileges belonging to him, for, after all, rights and duties go very much together.

At the first meeting of Kirk Session after a new minister has been inducted there is to be engrossed in the Minute a certified intimation of the induction which has been supplied by the Presbytery Clerk (p 88). Likewise, at the first meeting of Session after the occurrence of a vacancy, it should be recorded that the parish became vacant on ... by reason of ....

In virtue of his induction the minister is Moderator of his Kirk Session (or Kirk Sessions in the case of linking), he is a member of Presbytery and Synod, he is eligible for election as a commissioner to the General Assembly, and where the Model Constitution is in operation he is entitled, if he so wishes, to be Chairman of the Congregational Board.

Residence–In the years immediately following the Reformation the law was most strict in the matter of the absentee minister—understandably so. The law was so strict that for a minister to be absent from his flock for 40 days without reason

D

approved by the Assembly was declared to be adequate cause for deprivation. Today it is quite common for the Manse to be outwith the parish. Still, the Presbytery is entitled to insist that the minister reside within reasonable distance of his parish, and for any protracted absence he must seek permission in advance. Six weeks is the period generally accepted as the limit—if the absence is to be for longer the Presbytery must be consulted, when leave of absence will be granted and an Interim Moderator appointed. Should a minister absent himself from his parish without leave for longer than this he lays himself open to be treated as having absconded, and the penalty for that is deposition.

This in fact is the way to resolve the difficult situation that arises when a minister, perhaps in a fit of pique, 'resigns' and walks out without having sought or obtained from the Presbytery permission to demit; or when a minister simply vanishes—the lady organist having perhaps simultaneously vanished. If after due citation, which if his whereabouts are unknown will be made edictally in his Church, he does not appear to answer then he is held to be in desertion and is deposed.

Invariably when leave of absence is granted it is for a specific period, and during the whole of that time the Interim Moderator is in charge. Should a minister on leave for health reasons feel himself sufficiently recovered to resume before the expiry of the full period, he must apply to the Presbytery to discharge the Interim Moderator—he cannot at his own will return within the period of the leave (p 143).

Manse—The Manse is available to the minister for use in fulfilment of his ministerial functions and duties and for the accommodation of himself and his family. At one time it was his as a perquisite, but this is no longer so, and it is not available to him for letting. The Basis of Union of 1929 required that the minister shall reside in it unless with the express consent of the Presbytery he may reside elsewhere. The position in regard to Manses today is in a state of some uncertainty. My principal concern here is to emphasise that where a Manse is provided the minister is expected to occupy it. The Presbytery may grant him permission to live in his own house elsewhere and the congregation may be prepared to pay him a Manse Allowance, but if they have a suitable house to offer they are not under obligation to make such a payment. When, however, a Manse is not provided there must be paid a sum in lieu at the rate for Manse Allowance determined from time to time by the Maintenance of the Ministry Committee—at the time of writing it is £1500 per annum.

On the death of a minister a reasonable time will be allowed for his family to vacate the house. It is usual for the congregation to accept responsibility not only to keep the house wind and water tight but also to maintain a decent level of interior decoration.

Because he is held bound to occupy the Manse, the value of its occupancy is not chargeable for Income Tax. Where a house is held and owned by a congregation for the housing of its minister, there is a mandatory remission of 50 per cent of local rates, with permission to the local authority to make a larger remission. These benefits do not apply to a house owned or leased by the minister. Local rates are invariably paid by the congregation, but at the time of writing there is considerable uncertainty as to how ministers will be affected by the proposed new rating system. Representations on the subject are being made in high places.

The General Trustees operate a rule that unless in the most exceptional circumstances they will not authorise the purchase or erection of a house as a Manse which is of less than seven apartments—boxrooms not being counted as apartments.

Non-Intrusion—A minister's sphere of duty lies within the bounds of his own parish and he may move beyond these to perform ministerial functions only with the previous consent of the minister of the parish concerned, or on the order of the Presbytery or of a superior court, or to minister to members or adherents of his own congregation, or to conduct a marriage or a funeral by private invitation.

Access to Church Buildings—'The place of worship and other ecclesiastical buildings connected with every charge are at the disposal of the minister for the purposes of his office.' Further, he 'may use them or grant permission to others to use them for all purposes connected with the congregation or any of its organisations, and also for all purposes of an ecclesiastical, religious or charitable nature even if they be not connected with the congregation'. He may not use them, or grant the use of them, for any other purpose without the consent of the body responsible for the temporal affairs of the congregation.

The minister has sole power over the ringing of the Church bell, and, according to Mair's *Digest of Church Laws*, 'he is keeper of the Communion vessels and furniture, and is answerable to the parish if they are lost or put to any profane use'.

Public Worship

According to the *Westminster Confession*, public worship consists of prayer with thanksgiving, reading the Scriptures, preaching and hearing the Word, singing the Psalms, and the due administration and worthy receiving of the Sacrament; and God is not to be worshipped in any way 'not prescribed in Holy Scripture' (*Westminster Confession xxxi*). The only rule-book in this field is the *Directory of Public Worship of God* (1645) which, in its Preface, is at pains to point out that it is not to be treated as a liturgy, but as a base that allows the individual minister 'to furnish his heart and tongue with other materials of prayer and exhortation, as shall be needful upon all occasions'.

In a day when the Word is rarely being heard at home and very little at school it is doubly important that it should be read at public worship. While for many years the Authorised Version alone was in use, and while the Assembly have given their blessing to the New English Bible, there is no prescribed translation, and the choice here, as in so many aspects of the service, lies with the minister.

Book of Common Order–From time to time a *Book of Common Order* has been published bearing the imprint of the Church of Scotland—the most recent in 1979 replaced that of 1940 which in turn took over from the former *United Free Church* book of 1928 and the *Church of Scotland* book of 1923. The interesting point about all of these is that, while they were prepared at the behest of the General Assembly, and while their publication carries the blessing of that court, their content was never formally approved by the Assembly. In the case of the most recent book, for example, the relevant deliverance was in these terms: 'The General Assembly acknowledge the considerable work of the Committee in the production of the *Book of Common Order* 1978 ... and commend this publication to the whole Church'. In the Introduction to the volume, the Convener of the Committee on Public Worship and Aids to Devotion explains that a certain order is followed because 'the Committee believes that ...' and the passage concludes, '... it is an order which the Committee believes best reflects the logic of the Gospel'. The Assembly have never at any time declared their acceptance of this view of the logic of the Gospel, and there can be little doubt that many would challenge it.

The *Book of Common Order*, therefore, is a guide to ministers in the conduct of public worship, in the administration of the sacraments and in other services of the sanctuary—it is not binding upon anyone. As was said in the 1928 Book, a Service Book is necessary 'to express the mind of the Church with regard to its offices of worship, in orders and forms which, while not fettering individual judgment in particular, will set the norm for the orderly and reverend conduct of the various services in which ministers have to lead their people'.

Innovations in the Order of Public Worship—It is frequently said that the minister and he alone is in charge of the worship of his congregation. This is true to the extent that no-one else in the congregation has any standing in regulating the conduct of worship, but it is not true if it is meant to imply that the minister is absolute master in this field. It is the Presbytery which has to carry the ultimate responsibility for the conduct of worship in all the congregations within its bounds, and the Presbytery appoints each parish minister as its executive within his own domain. What this means is that on the one hand the Presbytery may call one of its ministers to account in regard to his discharge of this responsibility, and on the other hand that anyone who is dissatisfied with the way in which worship is being conducted in his congregation has to his hand a remedy in the form of a petition to the Presbytery.

The Act of Parliament of 1592 (the Magna Carta of the Kirk) deals with the matter of innovations, and the Assembly of 1866 construed the relevant section thus—'It belongs to the Presbytery to regulate matters concerning the performance of public worship and the administration of ordinances, in accordance with the laws and settled usages of the Church, and they are to take cognisance of the alleged existence or proposed introduction of any innovation or novel practice coming regularly to their notice, and after enquiry, if this appears necessary, are to give such deliverance as seems to be warranted by the circumstances of the case and the laws and usages of the Church; and it is their duty to enjoin the discontinuance or prohibit the introduction of any novel practice inconsistent with the laws and settled usages of the Church, or a cause of division in the congregation, or unfit for any cause to be used in the worship of God either in general or in the particular kirk'.

At least three points here are worthy of note. First that the Presbytery far from being merely empowered is put under obligation to deal with instances of unwelcome innovations; second that it is to do so when 'such matters come regularly to its notice' (and this would certainly happen were any person or group of people to present a petition); and third that the mere fact that the innovation is causing division within the congregation is declared sufficient ground for the Presbytery to order its discontinuance—it does not have to be proved that it is inconsistent with the settled usages of the Church, for that is another, and quite separate, ground for condemnation.

Who May Conduct—As has been said, the conduct of public worship belongs to the minister subject to the direction and control of the Presbytery, and the law is very strict as to whom he may allow to function in his stead. The matter was reviewed as recently as 1986 and according to an Act of that year the authorised persons are ministers (including auxiliary ministers and ministers of most other denominations), probationers, licentiates, regular students of divinity, deaconesses licensed to preach and approved candidates for such licence, lay agents recognised by the Department of Ministry and Mission, and readers. It is important to note that 'readers in training' is not a permitted class in terms of the Act. The employment of anyone outside these catagories is prohibited, except that in special circumstances someone not qualified as above, including an elder or elders of the congregation, may be invited to conduct the service. In any such case intimation is to be made to the Presbytery Clerk within 14 days.

The new Act further provides that, 'In an emergency when, for any reason, it becomes evident at or before the time appointed for public worship that the responsibility of the minister under this Act has not been discharged, it shall be the duty of the Session Clerk, failing the senior elder present, to lead the congregation in an act of devotion, or invite someone else to do so, and to report the circumstances to the Clerk of the Presbytery as soon as possible thereafter'.

It is quite common today for a service on some special occasion to be conducted by a group of Elders, or by the Woman's Guild, or by the Youth Fellowship. The legality of this is highly questionable, and in my view at the very least the minister should be present throughout and should nominally be in charge of affairs—if anything is done amiss it is he and not the perpetrator who will be held responsible.

Blessing the People—The *Westminster Confession* lays it down that one of the principal functions of the ministry is to bless the people. This may be seen as being fulfilled in the pronouncing of the benediction at the close of every service of public worship. For this reason it seems to me important that this should be a blessing and not a prayer—'be with you', not 'be with us'. And I regard as quite indefensible in this context, a practice which is coming into fairly common use of substituting for

the benediction what is called 'The Grace' whereby
all present repeat together the words of the
Pauline benediction, 'The grace of the Lord Jesus
Christ...'. Whatever attraction this may have
liturgically I cannot believe it meets the requirement that the minister should bless the people. For
myself I think the blessing should confine itself to
those who are there to receive it and that it should
not extend to absent friends however deserving—
but that, as I say, is a personal view.

The Sacraments

One of the things listed above as belonging to the
minister subject to the direction and control of the
Presbytery is the dispensing of the sacraments.
What that means is that no-one in the congregation
may dispense or have any say in how the minister is
to dispense or whom he may appoint to do so in his
place. The Assembly, however, has imposed certain restrictions in regard to the latter point.

Who May Dispense—The subject of who may
dispense the sacraments within a charge of the
Church of Scotland is governed by the terms of Act
IV of 1975. This distinguishes between the authority given for regular dispensation over a period
(*locum*, exchange, *etc*) and permission to do so only
on one single occasion (baptism by the child's
grandfather and that kind of thing).

Those entitled to dispense on the former basis
are:

(1) a minister of the Church of Scotland;

(2) a minister of the United Reformed Church or
of a Presbyterian Church whose doctrine is in

keeping with our own and who has been duly authorised by the Presbytery of the bounds—the authority to be given only in special circumstances of which the Presbytery is sole judge;

(3) a duly ordained minister of one of the Lutheran or Reformed Churches in Europe, of the Waldensian Church, or of the Church of the Czech Brethren—all with authority of the Presbytery as in (2) above; and

(4) an ordained minister of a non-Presbyterian Church who holds an appropriate certificate from the Committee on Probationers and Transference and Admission of Ministers—again with authority of the Presbytery as in (2) above.

A parish minister may on occasion invite a minister of another denomination whose orders are in accordance with the standards of the Kirk to administer one of the sacraments. This he may do completely on his own authority, but if the invitation is accepted the matter is to be reported in writing to the Presbytery Clerk within 14 days after the event.

Baptism

In 1953, in response to an Overture from the Presbytery of Glasgow asking for a fresh examination of the doctrine of baptism with a view to securing 'theological agreement and universal practice' with regard to this sacrament, the Assembly appointed a Commission which laboured for the next nine years over the production of a 'Statement of the Doctrine of Baptism'. Interim reports were remitted from time to time to Presbyteries for study and comment, until finally in 1962 the Statement was sent down under Barrier Act procedure, being passed by the following Assembly into a standing law of the Church. Along with it went down another Overture designed to translate the theology into terms of practice. They were called respectively 'anent the Doctrine of Baptism' and 'anent the Administration of Baptism to Infants'. Both Overtures were approved and merged into one Act—XVII of 1962—under the latter title. This is something of a misnomer since the doctrinal part of the Act covers the whole subject of baptism. It is this legislation which now governs the administration of baptism both to children and to adults.

Infant Baptism—There are only two sets of circumstances in which baptism is to be administered to a child—(1) where one or both parents have themselves been baptised and are (a) members, (b) *bona fide* adherents, or (c) 'desire to seek admission to full membership of the Church', or (2) where, the parents being unknown or having been separated from the child, the Kirk Session is satisfied that the child is under Christian care and guardianship. The parents or guardians who have to undertake the upbringing of the child are to receive such instruction in the meaning of baptism as the minister may deem appropriate. In connection with (1b) the Assembly in 1964 agreed that absence from public worship due 'to causes which render such attendance a practical impossibility' is not to be a barrier. In the case of (1c) an elder is to be appointed to shepherd the parents into full communion and to exercise pastoral care over the child.

A minister is not to baptise a child from another parish (unless the parents belong to his congregation) without consent of the minister of that parish; and where a minister has declined to administer baptism no other minister may do so without the consent of the Presbytery. It would seem, therefore, that when a minister is approached by people not known to him with a request for the baptism of their child he must first satisfy himself that an unsuccessful approach has not already been made to some other minister—it is not enough to presume this to be the case. If they are his parishioners, of course, the case is different.

Baptism is to be in the name of the Father, Son, and Holy Ghost, with water, and by sprinkling, pouring, or immersion. Other elements may not be used. Baptism is normally to be administered in Church, although this is not essential. The details regarding baptism are to be entered in the Baptismal Register of the congregation, and a Certificate of Baptism is to be issued. The Act makes no reference to this, but there is much to be said in favour of making an appropriate entry on the child's Birth Certificate recording the date and place of baptism and affirming that it was administered in water in the name of the Trinity. A Birth Certificate is much less likely to go amissing than a Certificate of Baptism, and ability to prove baptism can later be of considerable importance.

Change of Name—The name to be used in the Service of Baptism should, naturally, be the name or names entered on the Birth Certificate. If, however, the baptism occurs within 12 months of the date of birth, a change of name may, at the request of the parents, be effected in the name given at the time of registration, and baptism should be administered using the latter name— otherwise the change will not be accepted. It is for the parents, if they have not already done so, to obtain the appropriate form from the Registrar and for the minister to complete this. On its being returned (which must be within two years of the date of birth) the Registrar will enter the new name in the Register of Corrections.

Tinkers—In 1967 the Assembly adopted certain guidelines for the baptism of the children of tinkers. A request for such baptism should be seen as an opportunity for evangelism, and it is to be kept in mind that refusal could easily be interpreted as meaning that the Church was not interested in tinkers. 'Against this there is a considerable danger of an element of superstition being associated with the sacrament unless the teaching and practice of ministers deliberately guards against this. Every case would have to be regarded on its own merits. We would favour the administration of baptism whenever some kind of assurance of Christian upbringing could reasonably be given, and we would bear in mind that such assurance in the case of tinkers might not be quite what one would look for in the case of settled parishioners.' Baptism should be administered in Church at a service in the usual way, and even where this is not possible, 'it should at least take place in the Church, and, of course, by the parish minister'.

Baptism of Adults—Baptism may also be administered to adults, the only qualification being that the person must be prepared to make profession of sin and promise of new obedience. It is common for baptism to be so administered at the time when the person is seeking to enter into full communion with the Church. It is important to note that admission to Communion does not 'supersede' or 'include' baptism and that care should be taken to ensure that only those already baptised are accepted for admission. The two acts may fittingly be encompassed in the one ceremony. Careful instruction must, of course, be given to all applicants for such baptism.

Service of Blessing—I depart for a moment from the Act to say that while the Church of Scotland has accepted infant baptism as its norm, it has not insisted upon it as its rule. There are those in the Church who, while utterly commited to providing their children with Christian training and upbringing, are convinced that baptism is something to be consciously sought and accepted and that in consequence, believers' baptism is the proper course. Although, therefore, they will not seek baptism for their children they may well approach their minister with a request for a service at which they may give thanks for the gift of their child, seek a blessing upon it, and commit themselves to its Christian nurture. In such circumstances I imagine the minister would want to explain to them the tradition and significance of infant baptism, but if they remained unconvinced I am not aware of anything in the law or usage of the Church to prevent his acceding to their request, and I can see much to be said in favour of his so doing. In the light of the Caithness case he must certainly not encourage the adoption of this course (see hereunder).

'Second Baptism'—In 1976 there came to the General Assembly an appeal which raised a question regarding the propriety and validity of 'second baptism'. The circumstances were as follows. An elder who has been baptised as a child sought and received baptism at the hands of a minister of the Baptist Church. He appealed to the Assembly against a judgment of the Presbytery of Hamilton to the effect that he had erred in so doing. After a most interesting debate the General Assembly rejected the appeal, re-affirming the confessional belief, shared with the Universal Church and particularly with all branches of the Reformed Faith, that re-baptism is in violation of the doctrine of one baptism whether of infants or of believers, and of the article that baptism is administered but once to any person.

Again in 1981 there came to the Assembly a case from the Presbytery of Caithness, involving this time a minister and an elder. The Assembly found that the two men, by their acceptance of second baptism, had been guilty of repudiating the validity of their baptism as infants. A Special Commission of Assembly was appointed to meet with the Presbytery and the men concerned, the latter to be rebuked, and in the minister's case an undertaking was required that he would uphold the doctrine and practice of the Church of Scotland in regard to baptism of infants.

The Lord's Supper

Along with his general duty in relation to the administering of the sacraments the minister carries responsibility for the preparation of first communicants.

Confirmation—It has long been accepted in the Church of Scotland that the objective of the preparation which the minister is here seeking to provide is for the confirmation by the candidate of the vows taken on his behalf at the time of his baptism, and that this is a necessary prelude to his reception into the full communion of the Church. The *Directory* of 1592 has nothing to say about a Service of Confirmation or of Admission. At that time, and for long after, Kirk Sessions examined all members of congregations before each celebration of the Lord's Supper and decided whether or not they might be admitted to the table—the tables were 'fenced'. It was in the latter half of the last century that there was introduced an 'Order of Admission' in which first communicants made public confession of their faith. The *Order Book* of 1923 includes a 'Form and Order for the Confirmation of Baptismal Vows and Admission to the Lord's Supper'. What was in mind here, clearly, was the confirming of baptismal vows—the preamble states that having in infancy received baptism, 'you have now of your own choice come forward to acknowledge before God and His Church the covenant made on your behalf'.

To describe this as 'confirmation' while perfectly correct and proper can, unfortunately, easily lead to confusion with the 'confirmation' which can be conferred by a priest. This is illustrated by the fact that by the time of the *Book of Common Order* of 1940 the reference is to an 'Order for the Confirmation of Baptised Persons and for their Admission to the Lord's Supper'. By the book of 1979 the service had become simply 'Confirmation and Admission to the Lord's Supper', and, significantly, while the candidate is asked to subscribe to a confession of faith, he is not asked to confirm the vows taken at the time of his baptism. There has crept in (or has been subtly introduced) an identification of two utterly different things—confirming vows and confirming candidates. Exactly what is meant by the latter is made plain in a 1973 publication of the Committee on Public Worship and Aids to Devotion when it refers to confirmation as being 'what God does to those who have truly put their faith in Him and have committed their lives to him', and as meaning 'making strong'.

This latter, and very different, meaning of the word 'confirmation' does not appear at any time to have been specifically adopted by the General Assembly and ministers are therefore entitled—I think even bound—to believe that the confirmation for which they are to prepare candidates is something which is to be done *by*, and not something which is to be done *for*, and certainly not *to*, them. It is vows that are to be confirmed, not people.

Reception of Communicants—The minister having taken under special instruction in the truths of the faith all who would enter the full communion of the Church and having satisfied himself that they are all baptised persons, it remains for the Kirk Session to resolve that they should be received and have their names added to the Communion Roll of the congregation. The minister will then, in face of the congregation, put to the candidates the questions appointed, and on receiving satisfactory answers will in prayer receive them and commend them to the prayerful acceptance and care of the congregation. In 1935, and again in 1968, specimen questions were approved by the Assembly, but a great deal of latitude is allowed in this field.

Communion Service–The communion is celebrated by the minister—it is not dispensed by the Kirk Session, and it is not necessary that the court be constituted for the celebration. It is a custom of long standing that the elders assist the minister in the distribution of the elements, but there is no law requiring this to be so. At, say, a Dedication Service for the Woman's Guild it would be fitting and perfectly in order that Guild members should render this service. The minister is in full charge of the service, but it is the Kirk Session which determines the frequency and the times and seasons.

In 1690 the Assembly by Act X 'hereby discharges the administration of the Lord's Supper to sick persons in their homes, and all other use of the same except in the public assemblies of the Church'. No doubt this had its roots in the horror of idolatry that was so characteristic of the Church of that day—the idolatry being seen in the use of reserved elements. I am not aware that the Act has been repealed, but I think the practice of taking Communion to the sick can today be said to have become legally established by use and wont.

Marriage

Marriage was one of the sacraments of the Roman Catholic Church which was discarded at the time of the Reformation, but although it has not since then been regarded as sacramental in character, the connection between the Church and marriage has been both long and intimate. The law governing Scottish marriage changed little before 1940, but since then it has altered quite considerably.

Before 1940 – The historical situation in regard to marriage in Scotland was that there were two ways in which a couple could be wed—the regular and the irregular. The former of these was a marriage conducted by a minister of religion, the latter might take any one of three forms—declaration *de praesenti*, promise *cum subsequente copula*, or cohabitation with habit and repute.

Declaration *de praesenti* was in very popular use before it was abolished in terms of the Marriage (Scotland) Act of 1939—it had been the 'regular' form of 'irregular' marriage! It consisted simply in the parties taking one another as man and wife, usually but not necessarily in the presence of witnesses. It was simple enough in all conscience. But the introduction in 1855 of compulsory registration of births, marriages and deaths, introduced a complication—in order for such a marriage to be registered the fact of the exchange of consents had to be proved, and this was done by having a sheriff examine the witnesses, after which he gave authority for registration. The easiest way to achieve this was to have the whole affair encompassed in one comprehensive exercise. Hence the tendency for those so wed to claim (quite wrongly) that they had been 'married by the Sheriff'.

Promise *cum subsequente copula* (also abolished by the 1939 Act) was of very rare occurrence because the promise could not be established by parole evidence but only by writ of the defender and it was not likely that that would be available.

Cohabitation with habit and repute continues to this day. It refers to the case of a couple who are both free to marry and who have been living together as man and wife, being known to the world as such, but who have never gone through any formal ceremony. '"Habit and repute" arises from parties cohabiting together openly and constantly as if they were husband and wife, and so conducting themselves towards each other for such a length of time in the society or neighbourhood of which they are members as to produce a general belief that they are married persons.' The issue arises usually over a question of succession following on the death of one of the parties and the surviving spouse approaches the court with a view to having the marriage recognised. The cohabitation may have begun when one of the parties was not free to marry, but if it is persisted in after the barrier has been removed it will still be valid (Campbell v Campbell 1867).

Gretna Romances—In 1754 an Act was passed doing away with irregular marriages and making parental consent a necessity for the marriage of minors, but as this legislation did not apply to Scotland there grew up a positive trade in runaway marriages at Gretna Green and also at Lamberton Toll at Berwick and at the Bridge Toll-house at

Coldstream—although it was Gretna that was to capture most of the limelight. In fairly recent times Gretna provided a haven for under-age runaway couples from the continent. From the very beginning the whole affair was something of a scandal masquerading as romance, and the ultimate of stupidity was surely reached when couples travelled from Aberdeen to Gretna for the sake of being in Scotland and enjoying the benefit of Scots law! But old customs die hard, and though the smiddy may now be a mere museum, the Parish of Gretna must *per capita* have far and away the highest marriage rate in Scotland.

Civil Marriage–The Marriage (Scotland) Act 1939 considerably altered the position, particularly in that it provided a new form of regular marriage. It could be said to have introduced a new division into marriage—as between religious marriage and civil marriage. This latter was marriage contracted in the office of an authorised Registrar of Births, Marriages and Deaths. It demanded the same preliminaries as religious marriage (see hereunder) except that the Registrar would not accept a Certificate of Proclamation.

Preliminaries–Before a religious or a civil marriage could be celebrated certain preliminaries had to be gone through and a Marriage Schedule obtained from the Registrar of the District within which the marriage was to take place. There were three possibilities. The first of these was *proclamation of banns*, a custom of very ancient origin. In any Church situated within the Registration District where the parties had their normal residence or wherein they had resided for 15 clear days before application, at the principal service on one, two or three Sundays, intimation was made from the pulpit of the intention to marry and opportunity was provided for anyone to object. Proclamation could only be made in a charge of the Church of Scotland. It was customary for a proclamation of intention to marry to be made in a Roman Catholic place of worship, but this had no legal validity as banns. The second method was *Publication of Notice of Marriage*, which was introduced by the Marriage Notice (Scotland) Act of 1878 and which consisted in having a notice of the proposed union exhibited for eight days on a board outside the Office of the Registrar of the District or Districts of residence of the parties. The third possibility—*Licence*—was a creation of the 1939 Act. Where because of illness of one of the parties or other emergency neither of the above methods had been pursued, a joint application might be made to the Sheriff who could, if satisfied, grant a licence whose validity lasted for only ten days. It is not clear of what the Sheriff had to be 'satisfied' and it is difficult to imagine how illness or other emergency could have prevented the doing of things that would have had of necessity to be done before the emergency arose. It should be noted that this form of licence was utterly different from the licence and special licence which belong south of the border and which are granted by no less than the Archbishop of Canterbury.

Banns—In 1975 the General Administration Committee reported to the Assembly that in connection with the examination into the operation of Scots marriage law then being carried out by a Commission under Lord Kilbrandon, it had been represented on behalf of the Church of Scotland that in modern days neither proclamation nor publication enjoyed effective publicity-value and that a system of annotation of birth-entries coupled with a much more rigorous examination of the credentials of those applying for a Marriage Schedule would prove more effectual in preventing bigamous and other illegal unions. The Assembly ratified the action that had been taken. The new Marriage Act was passed in 1977 and as from the beginning of the following year the calling of banns and the publication of notices officially ceased. The proposal for the annotation of birth entries has, however, never been implemented, although in fairness it has to be conceded that no noticeable increase in bigamous unions has resulted.

Marriage (Scotland) Act 1977 — In conformity with the demands of a multi-racial society the scope of religious marriage has, under the 1977 legislation, been extended to embrace those of other faiths as long as monogomy is accepted and adequate vows are undertaken. In place of the former preliminaries the couple have now to present themselves at the Office of the Registrar within whose District the marriage is to be celebrated a fortnight to three months in advance of the crucial date, taking with them their birth certificates. The Registrar will issue a Marriage Schedule, and this must be in the hands of the minister before the wedding begins. Under the Act the minister is guilty of a criminal offence if he conducts a marriage service in the absence of such a Schedule. No matter what the pressures may be—from a swooning bride, a hysterical mother, or a threatening father, the minister must set his face as a flint against any kind of ceremony until the Schedule is in his hands.

Although proclamation is no longer a necessary preliminary to marriage in Scotland, and although Act III of 1978 repealed all earlier legislation concerning it, rescinding Schedules and Regulations relevant thereto, the same Act conserved the right for any person usually resident in Scotland to have banns proclaimed in his parish of residence if this would facilitate marriage furth of Scotland where evidence of proclamation is required. This will apply to marriages to be conducted south of the border in the Church of England where not only evidence of proclamation may be demanded, it *must* have been proclaimed on three separate Sundays.

Form of Service—Under the Act of Parliament it is left to ministers of the Church of Scotland to follow their own form of service, but the Assembly of 1977 passed a Declaratory Act setting forth the basic minima which the Church currently requires as essential to constitute a valid marriage service: first that the marriage is celebrated by an ordained minister in a religious ceremony wherein before God and in presence of at least the minister and two competent witnesses, the parties take each other for life as man and wife and are by the minister declared to be so; and second that the minister assures himself that the legal requirements have been met and that the parties know of no legal impediment, and that he ensures the due completion of the Marriage Schedule.

Legal Requirements—The legal requirements referred to above are that the persons are of age and are not related within the forbidden degrees. There is no need for parental consent in Scotland. The minimum age for marriage is 16, and some years ago the then Procurator gave the opinion that a minister should not celebrate a marriage until at least the day after the sixteenth birthday of the younger partner. To be a 'competent witness' the person must be at least 14 years of age and *compos mentis*. In the case where a party to a marriage is illiterate he should make a cross where the minister writes, 'John Bloggs X His Mark', and this should be subscribed by two witnesses, preferably not the same as those who are witnesses to the marriage.

When Married?—While it is important that the minister ensures the due completion of the Marriage Schedule, I am clear that this is not an essential constituent of the actual marriage but only of the registration of the marriage. Suppose, for example, that the bridegroom suffered a heart attack and died on the way to the vestry, there could be no signature and therefore no completion of the Schedule. I am quite clear, however, that in such circumstances there has been a marriage and that the bride is now a widow with all the legal implications in regard to property, pension, *etc*, which that condition carries. I am pretty sure the minister and the witnesses will need to appear before the Sheriff to testify to the fact that consent had been given and the couple had been declared married. On the strength of this, as I see it, the Sheriff will authorise the registration of the marriage in the absence of the completed Schedule.

Who May Celebrate—The Assembly have consistently resisted any attempt to allow other than an ordained minister to celebrate marriage. In a very few cases authority has been given to a lay missionary working on an island where there was no resident minister. The suggestion advanced in 1985, that a Probationer in course of his Probationary Year might be permitted as part of his 'supervised training and experience' to conduct a marriage service, was rejected. When a minister is to be involved in an extended exchange it can be an advantage, and is perfectly in order, for the Presbytery to 'authorise Mr AB, minister of the Church of PQ, to solemnise marriages according to the forms of the Church of Scotland'. Both Registrar General and local Registrar should be informed and furnished with an extract minute.

Place of Marriage—Civil marriage can be contracted only in the Office of an Authorised Registrar. There is no restriction on where religious marriage may be celebrated. For a very long time most Scots marriages took place either in the manse, at the home of the bride, or in the hotel or hall where the reception was later to be held. Today this is very rare, most marriages being celebrated in Church. Although the service is to be in Church it need not be a public occasion and the doors may be kept closed.

The Marriage Schedule specifies where the marriage is to take place. A problem can arise if through some emergency the locus has at the last minute to be changed. If, to take an example, a marriage fixed for a Saturday afternoon is complicated by the bridegroom being in hospital as the result of an accident—what is to be done? Provided the hospital is in the same Registration District as the place designed on the Schedule the marriage may proceed, the minister making appropriate alteration and signing the change as well as enclosing a note in explanation of the circumstances. Otherwise it is essential that the Registrar of the District (of the hospital) be found. The police may be able to help in the search for this official.

Should a minister be invited to conduct the marriage of non-Anglicans in England he should note that marriage can be celebrated there only in a place of worship registered for marriages (or elsewhere on special licence issued by the Registrar General) and that the Registrar must himself be present during the ceremony.

Ecclesiastical Marriage–I have throughout used the term 'religious marriage', for this I believe to be much preferable to the term 'ecclesiastical marriage' which made its appearance for the first time in the 1977 Act. It seems an unfortunate choice of term since the object of the Act is to give authority to marry to various religious groups some of which would be proud and insistent in their claim that they are not Churches.

Marriage of Foreigners–Marriages contracted in Scotland between foreigners, or between a foreigner and a British subject so long as they satisfy the requirements of Scots marriage law are valid throughout Her Majesty's dominions. A minister, therefore, is perfectly justified in going right ahead with the marriage service given that the proper schedule is put in his hand. He does

well, however, to remember that the wedding will
not necessarily be valid in the country to which the
bridegroom (he being the foreigner) belongs and
to which the couple may well be intending at some
time to remove. In the interest of his member (the
bride) and of her possible children he will do well
to get in touch with the consul or other diplomatic
representative of the groom's country and discover
whether the marriage will be recognised there. If
not he should warn the bride very seriously of the
possible consequences, although, of course, at the
end of the day the decision must be hers.

Re-Marriage of Divorced Persons—In the terms of
Act XXVI of 1959 a minister is at liberty to marry a
divorced person whose spouse is alive, but in so
doing he must carefully adhere to the following
requirements:

(1) He should not accede as a matter of course
but should carefully inform himself concerning
the life and character of the parties, the grounds
and circumstances of the divorce, the future facing
any children concerned, whether any other
minister has refused to celebrate, and regarding
the ecclesiastical affiliation of the parties.

(2) He must carefully consider the possibility of
scandal should he accede, and of doing spiritual
hurt should he refuse.

(3) He must assure himself there has been
repentance where guilt was involved.

(4) He is not required to solemnise such a
marriage against his conscience. Each Presbytery is
to appoint an Advisory Committee with a member
of which a minister who is in doubt or difficulty
may consult. (It was also required that the number

of such marriages should be annually reported in the Schedule of Persons and Agencies, but this was repealed by the Assembly of 1985.)

Funerals

The most recent law one can find on the subject of funerals comes from the Directory of 1645 which says, 'When any person departeth this life, let the dead body, upon the day of burial, be decently attended from the house to the place appointed for public burial, and there immediately interred without any public ceremony'. It adds, 'Howbeit, it is convenient that the company apply themselves to suitable conference, and that the minister, if he be present, seek to edify, as at other times'. Prayer at the grave, it was feared, could lead to, or be interpreted as, prayer for the dead—'some superstitious think that singing and reading of the living may profit the dead'.

The long-established custom of the Church is that, unless in very exceptional circumstances, a parish minister will conduct a funeral service, if this is asked for, in respect of any of his parishioners deceased. In a case where the minister feels that the life of the deceased was such as to make something of a mockery of Christian burial it is well for him to remember that there are relatives and friends who are in sore need of comfort (a need all the greater perhaps because of the character of their loved one) and that towards them he has a special pastoral responsibility. Indeed the occasion of death can produce an admirable entry to a house where otherwise there might have been scant welcome. From the point of view of this evangelical opportunity the follow-up can be of even greater importance than the conduct of the funeral service.

Cremation—Recent years have seen a vast increase in the use of cremation so that today in most city parishes burial is very much the rare occurrence and the country districts are following suit fairly fast. The switch from the graveyard to the crematorium has created at least three problems for the parish minister.

The first of these has to do with the seemingly simple business of fixing a time. The crematorium is liable to offer the undertaker a space on a take-it-now-or-it-won't-be-there basis, and in the limited time left for decision the latter may be quite unable to make contact with the minister. They may well decide to go ahead and accept the time offered. When the minister returns from a heavy day in Edinburgh to discover that a cremation has been fixed for an hour when he cannot possibly attend, he may well feel intensely annoyed. I am quite clear that a minister has a duty to conduct a funeral service: I am equally clear that he is not under obligation to attend a crematorium at an hour that has been fixed without his being consulted. Difficult situations can arise in consequence of all this. A friendly relationship with the local undertaker can go at least some way towards avoiding the awkward impasse, but the difficulty is still very real.

A second question may arise over the question of what kind of service should be conducted where. In the days of burial there was no such problem.

The service proper was conducted in the house (or perhaps the Church) and a fairly brief and standard committal service sufficed at the grave. Today we have a service at the house (in many city areas at a 'funeral parlour') followed by another at the crematorium. In both cases there is a measure of physical comfort and shelter unknown in earlier days and in most cases friends have been invited to attend either or both of these services. Obviously there should not be two complete funeral services —for the sake of the family if for no other reason —yet the simple committal designed for a wind or rain-swept graveside seems rather inadequate for the vast gathering assembled in the crematorium. For myself I think the perfect answer is for the service in the house to be confined to a purely private family affair with the kind of readings and prayers suited to such an audience and for the public funeral to be at the later occasion. But it is for each minister to work out his own solution.

The third difficulty affects ministers in remote country areas where a round-trip of anything from 100 to 150 miles may well be involved and where it is fairly certain that some kind of 'refreshment stop' involving a further couple of hours will be built into the programme. The amount of time involved in this is quite frightening. Again it is a problem which the individual minister has to resolve in the best way he can in light of all the circumstances.

The Instruction of the Young

The instruction of the young belongs to the minister under direction and control of the Pres

bytery. It is a duty which he shares with the Kirk
Session who, according to the Education Department's 1985 Assembly report, 'have to make
provision for systematic Christian education
through the establishment and maintenance of
such supervised learning opportunities as seem
appropriate to all ages and stages of development
of the young people'. The Session also acts along
with the minister in the appointing of the leader of
the Sunday School, and it has to approve the
appointment of Sunday School teachers.

The minister is 'head' of the Sunday School
(even when, as is almost invariably the case,
someone else acts as Superintendent). In this
divided responsibility there surely lies the possibility of trouble where, for example, the minister
as 'head' sees things differently from the Superintendent as 'leader', and both disagree with the
Kirk Session as 'supervisor'. As I see it, the minister
would have the final word at congregational level,
but the Kirk Session, if it took the disagreement
very seriously and was convinced that the minister
was wrong, would be entitled to reach its own
decision on how things ought to be done, and if the
minister indicated he was not prepared to fall into
line the Session could petition the Presbytery
under whose direction and control, it will be
remembered, the minister is acting.

Notarial Execution of Wills

The Church of Scotland (Property and Endowments) Amendment Act of 1933 (Section 13)
provides that 'a minister of the Church of Scotland

E

who has been appointed to a charge without limit of time or for a period of years to officiate as minister, shall, in any parish in which such charge or part thereof is situated, have the like power as regards the notarial execution of wills or other testamentary writings as is conferred by Section 18(1) of the Conveyancing (Scotland) Act 1924 on a parish minister acting in his own parish'. The Act further provides that a certificate by the Principal Clerk of Assembly stating the parish in which the charge of any such minister is situated will be accepted as conclusive evidence on that point.

What is this Power?—The power of notarial execution in this limited context is an authority to write out a will for a person who is blind, or illiterate, or too ill to be able to write. If such a will is to be valid, the utmost care must be taken to ensure that certain conditions are complied with. First, obviously, the person wanting to make the will must be blind, illiterate, or too ill to write. Second (and this is rather tricky), the minister must be acting within the civil parish in which his own ecclesiastical parish or part of it is situated—that is to say, he is strictly confined, but is not confined within the bounds of his own ecclesiastical parish, for his power extends over the whole of the civil parish and may indeed include a second civil parish should his own ecclesiastical area overlap in that kind of way. Third, the minister has to have the will written out, or typed out, and he has to read it over to the grantor in presence of two witnesses who must also hear or see him given authority to sign. Fourth, the minister is to add the docquet as shown hereunder. It is essential that this docquet be in the minister's handwriting. Fifth, he has then, in the presence of the grantor and of the two witnesses, to add his own signature to each page as well as to the docquet, being particularly careful that on the last page he adds the date of signing. (This can be of great importance as otherwise it may not be possible to establish that the will supersedes one of an earlier date.) Sixth, the two witnesses have now to sign in the spaces indicated, adding the word 'witness' after their names. And last, the minister may not be an executor, a beneficiary, a trustee, or have any other interest under the will.

Form of Docquet—The following is the form of docquet prescribed by the Conveyancing (Scotland) Act 1924 in the case where the grantor of the deed is blind or cannot write.

Read over to, and signed by me for, and by authority of the above-named A B (*without designation*) who declares that he is blind (*or is unable to write*), all in his presence, and in the presence of the witnesses hereto subscribing.

Signed by me at ... this ... day of ..., Nineteen hundred and ....

....
(*Minister's Signature*)
Minister of the Parish of ....

Signature .... Witness
Address ....
Designation ....

Signature .... Witness
Address ....
Designation ....

Custody of Will—When a minister has been asked to act in this way it may be well for him to have the will scrutinised by a solicitor in order to verify that it is all as it should be. If the grantor expresses a desire that the minister retain the will 'for safe keeping' he should treat the request sympathetically —for it may well suit next-of-kin (who usually have ready access to the house and effects immediately following upon a death) that the will should not be found. If he agrees to hold the document the minister should arrange that there be put amongst the grantor's papers a note to the effect that there is a will in his keeping.

Limitation—It is most important to note that the notarial power vests in the minister only for this limited purpose and that he has no authority to attest any document which requires to be sworn in presence of a Justice of the Peace or Notary Public.

The Courts of the Church

One of the prescribed questions to which, on his induction to a parish, a minister has to return a 'satisfactory answer', is couched in these terms— 'Do you acknowledge the Presbyterian government of this Church to be agreeable to the Word of God; and do you promise to be subject in the Lord to this Presbytery and to the superior courts of the Church, and to take your due part in the administration of its affairs?'

I have never felt sure what exactly was implied by the use of the phrase 'in the Lord' which appears in the promise to be subject to the Presbytery. Clearly it introduces some kind of reservation or qualification. I imagine it would be cited as justification for refusal to comply with some injunction which the person on whom it was laid claimed was to him offensive on conscientious grounds. For example, a modern Thomas Gillespie, if he were instructed to preach at the service of induction of someone to whose admission he took the gravest exception 'in the Lord', would consider he was not in breach of his vows if he failed to appear.

Be that as it may, there can be no reservation or qualification attached to the undertaking given by the inductee that he will take his due part in the administration of the Kirk's affairs. At the very lowest estimate this must mean faithful attendance at meetings of all Church courts of which he is a member—Presbytery, Synod and, from time to time, General Assembly.

The Presbytery—The minister of a parish, an associate minister, an ordained assistant, a community minister working within the bounds—all are entitled to a seat in the Presbytery, and on retiring on grounds of age or health or to facilitate readjustment, are entitled to retain their seats. As a member of the court a minister is expected to attend ordinary meetings with some regularity, to accept appointment as occasion arises to take part in Presbytery services, to undertake the duties of Moderator if elected, and to accept his fair share of the deputation and committee work which constitutes so large a part of the activity of the court of today. He has also to be available for nomination by the Presbytery to act on Assembly committees.

The Synod—Until fairly recently every minister

who had a seat in Presbytery had likewise a seat in the corresponding Synod. In 1981 new legislation was introduced whereby a Synod, given the concurrence of all the Presbyteries in its province, may elect to change this to the extent that only a proportion of Presbytery members will be members of the Synod, the proportion being determined by the Synod, the appointments being made by the Presbyteries, and the persons appointed serving for a four year period.

The same considerations apply as in the case of Presbyteries regarding committee-work *etc*, it being specifically provided that even where the Synod has resolved to adopt the proportional basis, it is to be 'entitled to appoint as representatives to committees of the General Assembly any person or persons who would have been eligible for such appointment before the approval of the said resolution'.

The General Assembly—The membership of the General Assembly is made up of commissioners appointed by Presbyteries up to one-fourth of the number appearing on their Rolls. It is, I think, universal practice for Presbyteries to operate some sort of rota whereby the duty of attendance at Assembly falls upon a minister at least once in every four years. Some rotas are based on congregations so that a minister may chance to be sent to Assembly in his very first year; others work on a list of ministers and the newcomer will, of course, be added at the end of the list. If appointed a commissioner to the Assembly, a minister is required in terms of his commission 'to attend all the diets of the same as he shall be answerable', and on his return he is expected to report his diligence.

There are ministers who take pride in the fact that they never attend the courts of the Church. They should realise that, in common with all forms of democratic government, Presbyterianism can function satisfactorily only when all who have a share in its operation accept the responsibilities and faithfully discharge the duties which the system lays upon them.

Extra-Parochial Activities

Civil Judicatories—Until fairly recently ministers were, under pain of deposition, forbidden to be members of any civil or criminal judicatory or of Parliament. Act XXVII of 1959 removed this disability and there is now no Church impediment to a minister being, for example, a Justice of the Peace, or sitting in Parliament (but see hereunder), or to his being a member of the House of Lords.

Acting as a Juror—In terms of the Jurors (Scotland) Act of 1925 all ministers were exempted from sitting on juries and therefore were never called for such service. This has been altered in terms of a recent Act which provides that ministers may be called as jurors but that if they do not wish to accept service they are automatically excused.[1]

Clergy Disqualification—It has been stated above that there is no impediment placed by the Church in the way of a minister wishing to sit as a Member of Parliament. There is, however, a civil disqualification banning ministers of any of the Established Churches and of the Roman Catholic Church, and that not merely from sitting as members but even from being candidates in a Parliamentary election. Before he can be nominated as a candidate, a minister of the Church of Scotland must relinquish not only his charge but also his status. This is serious enough if he gets himself elected, but what if he does not? There seems no reason why the national Church should be singled out for this disability. At the time of writing the matter is under discussion with the Library of the House of Commons. It would appear that the Church of England has a procedure whereby a clergyman may submit his resignation to his bishop in such a way that if elected his resignation is seen as having taken effect, otherwise it is regarded as being withdrawn. We were asked whether we could devise comparable machinery but indicated that since the trouble arose from a law which could not be justified, it would seem appropriate for the change to be made at that end. In 1985 the Assembly indicated a specific desire to have the civil law amended to remove this anomaly.

School Chaplaincies—These are in a class by themselves in that a minister is not appointed to a School Chaplaincy by the Presbytery or by any agency of the Church—he is invited to accept the position by the Head Teacher and he continues in office during the latter's pleasure. The parish minister, although he will usually be welcome as a visitor to the school has no built-in rights in the matter, and in particular he has no right *ex officio* to act as School Chaplain.

In-Service Training
Courses on various aspects of the work of the ministry are organised on a residential basis by the

Education for the Ministry Committee, opportunities being provided for ministers in parishes to enjoy the advantages of these. The Sectional Committee responsible for this training has consistently reported on the 'less than satisfactory recruitment' to these courses. In 1984, in reporting on the proven worth of the courses, the comment was offered that they are of value 'not least for the minister who claims to be "too busy to take time off" but for whom an opportunity to evaluate his or her ministry, its priorities, its motivation and its theological base might well be precisely what makes it worthwhile, necessary even, to take time off to be at a course'.

The Committee is prepared to meet the cost of attendance at a course, including board and accommodation, travel and pulpit supply fee, but at the same time Kirk Sessions are encouraged to share in the costs by making themselves responsible for the pulpit supply fee, or by making contribution towards the other expenses of their minister's attendance.

Further Development—At the Assembly of 1985 a motion was successfully proposed from the floor requiring the Education for the Ministry Committee to bring to the next Assembly 'proposals for some form of mandatory post-ordination training'. The following year the Committee reported that while they appreciated the value of a mandatory scheme and 'the opportunities it would afford for developing even more widely the range and nature of its courses to meet the needs of the much greater number of ministers that will be involved in courses', they felt that the warm co-operation of

Presbyteries was essential for the successful operation of any scheme of this kind. They accordingly asked for time to confer with Presbyteries. My understanding at the time of writing is that, in consequence of the meetings at Presbytery level, it has been decided to invite the Assembly to depart from the mandatory element and instead to authorise a widening and extending of the range of the courses. The Committee is convinced—surely rightly—that continuing study is a necessary feature of the life of any minister who hopes to keep abreast of the constantly changing industrial, social and moral world in which he has to work, and that while compulsion may be inappropriate, ministers should themselves recognise the urgent need to take advantage of the courses provided.

Note to Chapter 5

1   Law Reform (Miscellaneous Provisions) (Scotland) Act 1980, Schedule I.

6

Acting as Intermim Moderator

Everyone knows that a Kirk Session cannot meet without a minister in the chair to act as Moderator. For certain purposes it may be convenient for the elders to meet in an unofficial conclave, but the Kirk Session as such can be constituted only by a minister and may continue in official being only under his chairmanship. So it is when a vacancy occurs, or if for any reason a minister is to be absent from his parish for a period of longer than six weeks, that the Presbytery appoints one of its ministerial members to act as Interim Moderator of Kirk Session for the duration of the vacancy or for the period of leave of absence that has been granted. It is perhaps worthwhile setting forth in some detail the duties that will fall to the Interim Moderator, particularly in the vacancy situation. We shall look first at the position when the appointment is for a limited period of leave of absence and then at the situation when a vacancy is involved, although it should be made clear that these are not alternatives and that much of what is said regarding the former will be equally applicable in the latter case.

During Leave of Absence

Leave of absence may be granted for any one of a variety of reasons, and the responsibility falling upon the Interim Moderator will vary accordingly.

In Case of Exchange

It is of fairly common occurrence today that a minister of the Church of Scotland arranges an exchange of manses and duties with, say, a minister of the United Presbyterian Church in the United States for a period which may be of three months or thereby. This obviously has to be cleared with the Presbytery in advance, and it is wise when applying for leave to ask the Presbytery to agree that the visiting minister may dispense the sacraments and may conduct marriages according to the forms of the Church of Scotland. (Even if it is not envisaged that the occasion will arise for this to be necessary, it is good to have the option open.) If it is agreed that he should have authority to marry, then intimation should be made to both the Registrar General and the local Registrar. Their consent is not required, but they are entitled to know, otherwise the Marriage Schedule is certain to be challenged when returned to the Registrar after the ceremony and a fair amount of bother needlessly encountered

In a case of this kind the duties of the Interim Moderator will be quite minimal, and indeed his services may not be called upon at all. Only if a Session meeting is required is he likely to be involved. It is essential, however, that an Interim Moderator be appointed, for no-one knows what kind of crisis could arise demanding action on the part of the Kirk Session; and in any event the visiting minister is entitled to have the support and the availability for advice which only an Interim Moderator can supply.

In Case of Extended Holiday
It may be that the minister is going off, probably abroad, for a holiday, or perhaps for study, extending beyond the accepted six week period. Again consent of Presbytery is required, and if leave is granted an Interim Moderator will be appointed. In such circumstances it is for the minister in consultation with the Interim Moderator to make arrangements for the maintenance of the work of the parish during his absence. This he may do by engaging a locum who will be responsible for both pulpit and pastoral duties; if there is an Assistant, arrangements may be made to cover the supply of the pulpit, the Assistant attending to the necessary pastoral work; or it may be that agreement is reached whereby pulpit supply is engaged and the Interim Moderator accepts responsibility for the pastoral duties. In this last case the responsibility for meeting the out-of-pocket expenses of the Interim Moderator will lie not with the congregation as in a vacancy, but with the absent minister. It is most desirable, whatever arrangements are made that a clear and firm programme is prepared, that the financial implications are carefully worked out (preferably also written out), and that key people such as the Session Clerk and the Kirk Treasurer know exactly who is responsible for what. It is essential that anyone in the congregation in need of pastoral

services may, without difficulty or delay, be directed to the right person.

In Case of Illness

If because of illness a minister is incapacitated and cannot carry out his duties for longer than six weeks, the Presbytery will grant leave of absence and will appoint an Interim Moderator. In such a case leave is always granted for a specific period—a number of months—it is never given on an indefinite basis. Of course it can always be renewed for a further period of three months or whatever. A personal problem can sometimes arise here. It may be clear to all most intimately concerned that there is little or no hope that the minister will be back on duty within perhaps a year, and yet it would be a serious blow to the invalid's morale to know that this was so. In such a case a much shorter period will be stated and extensions given.

Clearly the duties of the Interim Moderator are in this case much more onerous. It may be that the minister's condition is such that arrangements for the carrying on of the work can be made in consultation with him, although it is best that he should be regarded as fictionally absent and that the Interim Moderator should both assume and accept full responsibility. This will involve consultation with the Kirk Session regarding pulpit supply and so on. The Interim Moderator will preside at any congregational meetings that have to be held, and if the Model Constitution is in operation and the minister had acted as Chairman of the Board, then the Interim Moderator may act in his stead, although it is in order for a member of the Board to act in this capacity during the period of the leave.

A problem can sometimes arise in this kind of situation when the minister of the parish improves considerably in health and insists on trying to get back into things. He feels he should be doing this probably partly with a view to lightening the burden of the Interim Moderator who, after all, has his own parish and his own worries, and partly with a view to testing his recovered strength. What in fact such a minister is doing is adding to the worries of the Interim Moderator who no longer feels completely in charge of the situation. It cannot be too strongly emphasised that leave of absence is what it says, and that although he may be physically present in the parish a minister on leave is just not there so far as the parish and its affairs are concerned.

Should a minister on leave because of health, make a considerable recovery so that he feels perfectly fit to resume his duties before the expiry of his period of leave (and his doctor agrees with him in this), his course is to approach the Presbytery Clerk and arrange that the Presbytery will formally terminate the leave and thank and discharge the Interim Moderator. Until this has been done, the Interim Moderator is wholly responsible for the parish and its well-being, and it is only fair that he be allowed to get on with it without interference, however well-intentioned, from the Manse.

In the case of leave on acount of illness, the same options are available as above—a *locum tenens* to undertake all the duties, or pulpit supply with the Interim Moderator seeing to the pastoral side.

Financial—In the past when leave was granted on grounds of health, the Presbytery made itself responsible for the supply of the pulpit and made the Interim Moderator responsible for all else. The Presbytery did its part by impressing neighbouring ministers on a rota basis to preach in the Church affected, the hour of service being altered to allow this additional duty to be undertaken. Clearly this was far from an ideal arrangement and most Presbyteries instituted a Sick Supply Fund supported from Presbytery dues and capable of defraying the cost of pulpit supply in cases of illness. The position today is materially different from what it was then, in that the sick man is in receipt of payments from National Insurance, and some arrangement has to be made regarding the payment of the pulpit supply. A minister's income today should not be affected because he is ill, but equally he should not have a higher income when sick than when well. Nor should the Interim Moderator be allowed to be out of pocket.

During a Vacancy

A vacancy in a congregation may occur in any one of a variety of ways—by the death or deposition of the minister or by the severance by the Presbytery of the pastoral tie, by the translation of the minister, or by his demission of his charge. At the first opportunity after a vacancy caused by death or deposition (both of which are equally immediate in effect), the Presbytery appoints one of its ministerial members (not being a member of the vacant congregation) to act as Interim Moderator of Kirk Session during the vacancy. At the Presbytery meeting (at which steps are finally taken which will result in the creation of a vacancy under any other of the conditions mentioned), the Presbytery similarly appoints an Interim Moderator, but this time to act in the anticipated or prospective vacancy. The minister appointed in this latter way enjoys full powers as Moderator of Session in the conduct of all business (including readjustment business) connected with the forthcoming vacancy, although the parish minister is still in charge and carries full responsibility for all normal affairs. When the charge is a linked one, the Interim Moderator holds office in both (or all) Kirk Sessions involved.

Prospective Vacancy—Prior to 1960 no single step could be taken towards filling a vacancy until that vacancy had actually become a fact. It could be intensely frustrating to have to wait, for example, until the date of a man's demission, before one could begin doing things that could well have been going ahead without hurt to anyone's interest. A vacancy takes long enough to fill without deliberately wasting time. So in 1960 an Act provided for an Interim Moderator, in such a case, taking charge and moving forward with the preliminary business. In particular, readjustment negotiations may proceed, the Electoral Register may be prepared, and steps may go on up to and including the election of the Vacancy Committee. At that point, appeal may be taken to the Presbytery to proceed further; that court being at liberty, if satisfied this would be in the best interest of the congregation, to grant such permission. But in no circumstances is a nomination to be reported to the Kirk Session before the charge has actually become vacant.

While there is considerable advantage in getting the preliminaries out of the way while the sitting minister is still 'sitting', there can be real (and very obvious) dangers in proceeding too far in that kind of set-up. Each case has to be judged on its own merits and the guidance of a level-headed Interim Moderator can be invaluable at this stage.

Duties—It is the duty of the Interim Moderator to preside at all meetings of Kirk Session and at all meetings of the congregation at which the minister would have presided had the charge been full. When a congregational meeting has been called by the Presbytery in connection with readjustment, the Interim Moderator constitutes the meeting and then relinquishes the chair in favour of the Presbytery representative, but he attends the meeting and has the right to speak (although not to propose a motion). In certain circumstances, indeed, he may feel it is up to him to act as spokesman for the congregation and to present their case in the most convincing terms. And he may feel he has to do so even though he himself is not satisfied it is the right case. After all, he is not acting as judge but only as advocate, and the congregation is entitled to have its position fairly presented.

The arrangements for the supply of the pulpit throughout the vacancy are the responsibility of the Interim Moderator in consultation with the

Kirk Session and (in respect of payment) with the Finance Court. As in other cases arrangements may be made for a *locum tenens* who will be engaged on the basis (a) that he will to the fullest extent supply the want of a settled minister, (b) that he will conduct services, take marriages and funerals, and keep in touch with the sick and the aged, or (c) that he will take the services and conduct funerals when required. The financial terms will, naturally, reflect the amount of work to which the locum is committed. In so far as he may do so consistently with his other duties, the Interim Moderator is expected to supply the want of a settled ministry throughout the vacancy.

Cost of Pulpit Supply—In the case of a congregation whose stipend is paid partly in the form of 'aid' from the Minimum Stipend Fund or where any substantial part comes from teind or other endowments not held locally, the Assembly's Committee on the Maintenance of the Ministry is prepared to make payment towards the cost of pulpit supply during a vacancy in proportion to the amount of stipend coming from either or both of these sources during the last year of the previous incumbency. In most cases the Committee will be prepared on the same terms to subsidise a locum arrangement, but the Secretaries should be consulted and their concurrence obtained before any firm engagement is entered into. When the bulk of the stipend comes in aid, a system designed to help local cash-flow applies whereby vouchers may be obtained from the Department, one of which is given to the 'supplier' who cashes it at the Church Office—all provided an undertaking is given that the normal contributions to the Maintenance of the Ministry will continue to be forwarded throughout the vacancy.

'Preaching the Kirk Vacant'—The date of the vacancy is the day when the minister dies, is deposed, is inducted to another charge, demits office, terminates under terminable tenure, or has his pastoral tie dissolved, as the case may be. On the first convenient Sunday thereafter, pulpit intimation has to be made that the charge has become vacant on a certain day, and for what reason. It is not necessary that the Interim Moderator should make this intimation in person, but there is much to be said for his taking this opportunity of introducing himself to the congregation. In my opinion, whether the vacancy is real or anticipated this intimation cannot be made until it has actually occurred.

Preliminaries

Before the Vacancy Committee can be elected there are a number of important preliminary matters to be disposed of, and it is for the Interim Moderator to take a lead in seeing that these are attended to.

Electoral Register—An up-to-date register of the congregation is a *sine qua non* of any effective steps to fill a vacancy, and is also very valuable should voting have to take place on any issue of readjustment. So its preparation does not need to await the readjustment problem being resolved. As soon as possible, therefore, the Interim Moderator causes intimation to be made that on a certain day not less than 14 days distant, the Kirk Session is to meet in connection with the preparation of the Electoral Register and calling for the lodging of Disjunction Certificates and of Adherents' Claims before that date. The Register, which is a consecutively numbered list in alphabetical order of all who have a right to vote, having been thus prepared, is made available for inspection, and intimation as to when and where it will be on show is given on one Sunday. The intimation will also state when the Session is to meet to finish the job and invite anyone with an interest to appear then. It is perhaps worth mentioning that names on the Supplementary Roll have no right to be included on the Register. The Register having been finally adjusted, a docquet is added attesting it in the name of the Session as containing the names of so many members and so many adherents, and this is signed by Interim Moderator and Session Clerk. There is no appeal from a decision of Kirk Session in any question regarding the Electoral Register.

It is now for the Interim Moderator to ensure that the Register thus attested is conveyed to the Presbytery Clerk for attestation in the name of the Presbytery, and a duplicate copy is to be lodged with the Presbytery Clerk for retention.

It is important too for the Interim Moderator to ensure that no name is removed from the Electoral Register unless a written request for a Disjunction Certificate has been received (and the letter retained) by the Session Clerk. And, of course, to ensure that no name is added. Should more than six months elapse between the completion of the Roll and the congregation getting permission to call, the Kirk Session has power, if it so desires, to revise and update the Register in the form of an Addendum.

Readjustment—It is most unusual today for any congregation completely to escape the readjustment net, so while the Register is being prepared negotiations will most likely be proceeding with the Presbytery's Readjustment Committee regarding the future pattern for the congregation. This can be very time-consuming, and there are two directions in which the Interim Moderator can be of help. First, he can keep in touch with the Convener of the Presbytery Committee and make sure that no time is lost in the fixing of meetings, missing Presbytery meetings for reports, and so on. And second, by seeing that the local office-bearers face up to the realities of today's situation in a positive and realistic fashion. Readjustment is now a fact of ecclesiastical life and the wise course is not that of resisting it at all costs, but of ensuring that it will take a helpful form that, at the end of the day, will be to the advantage of all concerned.

Permission to Call—This, at one time called the *congé d'élire*, will be given when agreement has been reached by the Presbytery and the Assembly's Committee (a) that the congregation is to be served by a minister (with or without restriction or on terminable tenure), (b) that some form of readjustment has been, or is about to be, effected which will result in the creation of a congregation which is to have a minister, or (c) that a deferred union or linking has been agreed and that the vacant congregation is to have a minister right away who will later be minister of the united or linked charge.

Presbytery Advisory Committee—In terms of the 1984 Act the Presbytery, at the same time that it gives permission to call, is to appoint a Committee of three, of whom at least one is an elder, to meet with the Kirk Session (or with the Kirk Sessions jointly in a case of linking) to consider together the kind of ministry best suited to the needs of the charge. This Advisory Committee is to meet later with the Vacancy Committee once that is appointed and is then to confer with the Edinburgh Committee on Probationers and Transference and Admission of Ministers which will in due course send a list of four names for consideration by the Vacancy Committee. These are not in any condition of privilege, but it is expected that they will be accepted in good faith and that the Committee will 'afford to the candidature of those so nominated the same degree of careful and prayerful consideration as they accord to those of their own choosing'.

Vacancy Schedule—Also simultaneously with permission to call being given, a Vacancy Schedule is forwarded from the Assembly's Maintenance of the Ministry Committee to the Congregational Treasurer. It is for the Interim Moderator to arrange with the Presbytery's Maintenance of the Ministry Committee that a delegation meet with the local Financial Board to discuss the completion of this Schedule. This should be removed out of the way as soon as conveniently possible, for it is an advantage to be able to say to candidates right away what exactly the financial arrangements are; and, at the extreme end, no settlement of a minister can take place until the Schedule has been approved by both Presbytery and Assembly Committee.

The Vacancy Committee

By this time the congregation is in a position when it can proceed to elect a Vacancy Committee. Should it be a linked charge, or should a union be about to be effected, each congregation will have to meet separately and elect up to an agreed proportion of the total Committee. If a union has just been effected, it is still a good idea that the two former branches should meet separately and elect according to an agreed division. Generally the election is conducted at a meeting held after Morning Service—two Sundays' notice having been given—and the Interim Moderator should preside. Where two separate meetings have to be held, there is an advantage in having them held simultaneously, and to achieve this it will be necessary for the Interim Moderator to give a mandate to a fellow-minister to conduct one of the meetings.

Method of Election of Minister—Care must be taken by the Interim Moderator to ensure that in the excitement of electing the Vacancy Committee the other vital issue is not overlooked, for the congregation has also to decide at this point whether the election of the new minister is to be at an open meeting or by ballot. It can be quite a good idea to dispose of this question as the first item of business. In a case of linking, of course, the question does not arise since the election must of necessity be conducted by ballot.

First Meeting—The Vacancy Committee should meet briefly as soon as convenient after its election (at the close of the congregational meeting, perhaps) so that it may appoint a Convener, Vice-

Convener, and Clerk. The Interim Moderator has to call this meeting and preside over it. He must make it clear too, that he will always be available to sit as an assessor and to advise the Committee. Should the Committee so desire, and should he be agreeable, the Interim Moderator may act as Convener of the Vacancy Committee, but he has no vote either deliberative or casting. Convening a Vacancy Committee can prove quite a tricky exercise, for the possibilities of their getting into a fankle are both many and varied—not to say ingenious in some cases. In fairness it has to be conceded that in the nature of things in the average congregation the opportunities of gaining experience in this field are not very great. If there is a good strong character on the Vacancy Committee, by all means let him be the Convener, but if the Committee feels it wants the Interim Moderator, he should, in my opinion, accede to that request, recognising at the same time that if it is to be done properly the job will occupy a lot of his time. The Committee is at liberty to employ a Clerk who is not of its number, but I feel a happier solution is for a member of the Committee to accept on the understanding that he is free to employ an amanuensis.

Procedure—There are a number of matters connected with the procedure of the Vacancy Committee which are governed by statute, but there are also many issues where the Committee must be guided by its own good sense and feeling for the fitness of things. The Moderator should impress upon the members the need for confidentiality. A number of questions have to be answered early on.

They have to consider, for example, how a list of candidates is to be prepared, whether or not they are to advertise, how they are to go about hearing people in whom they are interested, and, something which seems often to be overlooked but which one hopes the meeting with the Presbytery Advisory Committee may highlight, they have to make up their minds exactly what they are looking for.

When it is desired to hear someone from far away, the Interim Moderator should be able to help by arranging for a local pulpit to be put at his disposal, by ensuring that he is properly accommodated and generally looked after during his visit, and that he is fully reimbursed for his outlays. If the candidate appears to be a serious contender, the Interim Moderator would do well to take the opportunity of showing him around the premises and giving him any information he may wish so that should he be invited to accept nomination he is, to that extent, *au fait* with the local situation.

Nomination—This consists in the choice of a name or names to be put up to the congregation for election, and it involves as a first step the submission to the Interim Moderator in his capacity as Moderator of Session a Minute setting forth the facts. Before this is done steps should have been taken to secure any necessary certificates to clear the person concerned: in the case of a Probationer the permission of the Committee on Probationers; in the case of a minister of another denomination or of a Minister Without Charge, a Certificate of Eligibility; and the appropriate Certificate from his Presbytery in the case of a minister in a first charge who has not completed five years there. If there is any doubt at all regarding a candidate's eligibility, this must be completely cleared before nomination is announced. The Presbytery Advisory Committee is to be informed as soon as a nomination has been agreed.

Election and Call
When the stage of nomination has been reached, the business passes out of the hands of the Vacancy Committee into those of the Kirk Session who are responsible for organising and overseeing the election. This will involve arranging for the nominee to preach, or, where there is a leet, for all the nominees to preach—on consecutive Sundays if at all possible. Where there is a leet, particular care must be taken to avoid any unfairness—or anything that could possibly be construed as less than scrupulously fair—in the arrangements made for each individual being heard.

Normally it is for the Interim Moderator to preside at all meetings connected with the election, but should he be unable to do so he may appoint another ministerial member of Presbytery to act in his place, provided he is not a member of the vacant congregation. He may have the assistance of other ministers in the conduct of a ballot vote. In the case of a deferred union or linking where one of the congregations already has a minister, it is for the Interim Moderator to consult with him in regard to arrangements for the nominee preaching in that church and for the conduct of that part of the election.

Election—When procedure is to be by open vote

this will be taken at a congregational meeting presided over by the Interim Moderator who will simply put the question, 'Elect Mr AB or not?' The votes will be counted (whether contested or not), the result recorded in the Session Minutes, and a Declaration of the Result completed and signed by the Interim Moderator. If there is a leet, at least a week must be allowed to pass between the last preaching and the meeting to elect. The names of the candidates are put forward and voted on in the order in which they preached. Voting continues, dropping the lowest, until one name emerges with a clear majority of votes cast, and the simple question is then put, 'Elect Mr AB or not?' In either case, in the event of a 'Not' decision the Interim Moderator has to issue a declaration that there has been Failure to Elect.

When it has been agreed that the vote will be by ballot, arrangements will have been timeously made to secure a supply of voting-papers in the approved form. At the polling-station the Interim Moderator or his designate sits with a copy of the Electoral Register and ticks off the names of everyone to whom a voting-paper is issued, but no identifying mark is put on the paper. If more than one congregation is involved, voting will, of course, take place at more than one point. As soon as practicable, and at the latest within 24 hours after the close of voting, the Kirk Sessions is—or the joint Kirk Sessions are—constituted by the Interim Moderator who then proceeds in the presence of the elders to count the votes. The first step in the case of a linking is thoroughly to mix the contents of the two ballot boxes. In the case of the sole nominee a Declaration of the Result of Election or of Failure to Elect is duly completed and signed by the Interim Moderator.

Where there is a leet the voting-paper provides for an indication of first, second, third, and so on, choices, so counting has to continue until one has emerged with a clear majority of votes cast when he is declared elected. Should there have been a majority of votes 'Against Any of the Above', the Interim Moderator will, inevitably, declare Failure to Elect. Admittedly the procedure is cumbersome and takes a lot of time, but it represents an improvement, surely, on the system as it was before 1984 when, if needs be, a second, third and fourth election might have to be held, each being preceded by pulpit intimation and being held 'not sooner than the Thursday and not later than the Tuesday next following after the intimation'. In a hotly contested case it must have helped to make the winter seem short!

When a ballot election has been concluded, it is for the Interim Moderator to seal up the voting-papers and stubs along with the ticked-off copy of the Electoral Register and to transmit these along with the other relevant documents to the Clerk of Presbytery. All of the papers are to be destroyed by the Presbytery Clerk after the person elected has been inducted—from which it follows that any challenge to the regularity of the procedure must have been made and disposed of before induction.

Frustrated Procedure–From all of the foregoing it must be obvious that there are a variety of ways in which things may go wrong—there can be withdrawal by the candidate at a number of stages or there can be failure to elect for a variety of reasons. When a contingency of this sort arises, it is for the Interim Moderator—as soon as at all possible and after two Sundays' notice—to call a congregational meeting when he may report on the situation that has arisen and discover whether the congregation wishes the same Vacancy Committee to start afresh (assuming they are prepared to do so) or not; and in the latter case to appoint a new Vacancy Committee which will start from scratch. It may be that the Vacancy Committee is quite prepared to try again, and they may do so on their own authority, but even if they are happy to do this I think there is much to be said for holding a congregational meeting and securing for them a clear new mandate. The law in fact provides that where there has been Failure to Elect, or where the candidate elected has declined, a requisition signed by not less than one-tenth of those on the Electoral Register may, within one week of the intimation of the failure or declinature, be lodged with the Interim Moderator requiring him to call a meeting of the congregation to decide whether to continue with the present Committee or to elect a new Committee, and in the latter case to go on and so elect. The fact that such a requisition was made would seem to indicate that the Committee no longer enjoyed the confidence of the entire congregation and might well lead to their refusing to continue.

Ius Devolutum—This is a carry-over from the days of patronage when the heritor's right to present expired unless an appointment had been made and the presentee inducted within six months of the vacancy having occurred. The right then reverted to the Presbytery. In the 18th century it was not uncommon for patrons deliberately to allow this to happen rather than face the unpleasant consequences that so often followed upon their exercising their right of presentation. The position today is that at the end of six months, if an end to the vacancy is not clearly in sight, the Kirk Session makes an approach to the Presbytery with a request for an extension of time, and a further three months is granted as a matter of course. If the matter is then still unsettled, a further extension may be allowed, but this time it will be only for sufficient cause shown. If extension is not granted the Presbytery acquires the right to raise afresh the question of readjustment before it is bound to go on and itself find a minister for the parish.

The exercise by the Presbytery of this right (or, to be more accurate, the discharge of this duty) is likely to arise in a congregation where there has been a complete division of opinion and things have reached a stage where it is unlikely that any Committee would be willing to act, or, even if they were, that they would carry the confidence of the whole congregation. So it is 'over to the Presbytery' which will make a choice of a person deemed suitable, and will do so on the recommendation of a strengthened Presbytery Advisory Committee. The Presbytery Clerk will then arrange with the Interim Moderator for the nominee to conduct worship in the vacant pulpit after due notice, and the congregation will be encouraged to sign a call in the usual way—but without any election, formal or otherwise. Thereafter procedure will be along normal lines.

Benefice Register

There also falls upon the Interim Moderator a most important duty connected with the Benefice Register—a duty, I fear, observed more in the breach than in the observance. An Act of 1931 requires that the Presbytery maintains a Benefice Register containing, in respect of each of its charges, an up-to-date entry detailing all property of every description belonging to that congregation, and indicating in whose custody it is, or with whom the titles to it are lodged. While heritable property and trust funds are especially in mind, there are usually various articles of value and significance as well as important books and records which are in the care and under the control of the minister.

During a vacancy, the Act decrees, the Interim Moderator is to cause an inventory to be made of all such properties which had been in the custody of the former minister and check that it is all there. He is also to have the inventory compared with the entry in the Presbytery's Register. He has to make arrangements for the safe keeping of these articles and volumes throughout the duration of the vacancy, and when the new minister is installed he is to ensure that a copy of the inventory and the articles listed therein are handed over to him. Within three months of his induction the new minister is to report to the Presbytery that this has been done and that the articles are now in his keeping.

Settlement

Assuming that the election has been satisfactorily

concluded and that the person elected has supplied the appropriate letter of acceptance, steps have to be taken in connection with the signing of a Call (*p* 83). The papers are now passed to the Presbytery which has to sustain the Call. Responsibility now passes into the hands of the Presbytery and all that remains is for the person elected to be inducted—ordained and inducted if he is a probationer. This is dealt with on page 85.

Discharge of Interim Moderator—At the close of the Service of Induction of a new minister, the Presbytery resumes its sitting when it is agreed that the new minister's name will be added to the Roll of Presbytery, and when the Interim Moderator is thanked and discharged. Thus his duties, which are likely to have extended over the best part of a year, are officially brought to a close.

One duty—however unofficial—still remains for him to perform. At the Congregational Social of Welcome, the Interim Moderator takes the chair and opens the proceedings, relinquishing his place in favour of the new minister after the latter has been welcomed in the name of the congregation and—if the old tradition still prevails—has been presented with pulpit robes.

The Interim Moderator is not entitled to any payment in respect of his services, but he must be able to recover out-of-pocket expenses, which can be considerable and which certainly should be claimed. It is customary at some point in the Welcome Social to give an expression of thanks to the Interim Moderator and to make him a presentation of some sort.

7

Support for the Ministry

Support for the minister in the work of his parish comes in a variety of shapes and sizes—as pulpit supply, in the form of assistance (which is of many different kinds), through lay missionaries, and through the diaconate. We shall look at each of these in turn.

Pulpit Supply

A minister is entitled in the course of a year to six Sundays of holiday supply, and also to have his pulpit supplied on the occasion of his attending the General Assembly when appointed a commissioner thereto. To qualify he must be absent from his pulpit on these Sundays—that is to say, he cannot deny himself the holiday, perform his own pulpit supply, and claim the fees.

Supply by Ministers, etc

The responsibility for organising pulpit supply on a national scale lies with the Committee on Probationers and Transference and Admission of Ministers; but, of course, ministers, interim moderators, and session clerks are free to make their own arrangements—as they frequently do. If, as a result of holidays, sickness, or other cause, or during a vacancy, pulpit supply is required, the rules governing those who may be engaged must be strictly adhered to. A list of those authorised to conduct public worship is contained in an Act of 1986, all as set forth on page 104.

Supply Agents–Application may be made to one of the Supply Agents appointed by the Assembly Committee, of whom there is one in Edinburgh, Glasgow, Aberdeen and Dundee. These agents are under instruction to keep lists of those they employ, indicating whether they are ministers, licentiates, deaconesses licensed to preach, deaconesses in training for licence, lay agents recognised by the Department of Ministry and Mission, readers, or ministers of other denominations; and the Committee is to examine these lists annually and to report thereon to the General Assembly. The Agents are further instructed that in allocating engagements preference is to be given to (a) probationers, (b) ministers without charge, and (c) students duly accepted as candidates for the ministry who have completed two full sessions of their theological course; and that no unauthorised person is to be employed.

Notes—(a) In view of the new connotation of 'probationer' as applying exclusively to persons engaged in their probationary year (*p* 39) and since such persons are unlikely to be available to take supply, I assume that in the second paragraph the words 'licentiates or probationers' should be substituted. (b) 'Ministers without charge' must, I think, be taken to include retired ministers. (Indeed there is some resentment that ministers who have gone into secular employment because they have lost faith in the parish ministry should be regularly supplying pulpits within that ministry.) (c) It is to be presumed that 'unauthorised' means not falling within any of the groups listed above. In the Reports for 1985 it was stated that 'the Committee continues to appoint representatives to visit the Agents, primarily to assure them of the gratitude and good will of the Committee for the work they carry out, but secondly to ensure that the work is carried out in accordance with the regulations of the General Assembly'.

It used to be that both the congregation asking for and the person providing the supply was charged a small Office Fee, but in 1978 the Assembly agreed that this practice should be discontinued and the service be provided free of charge.

Supply Fee–The General Assembly of 1982 approved amended regulations governing fees and expenses for pulpit supply as follows:

(1) The fee to be at the rate of 3p for every £10 of current stipend, no notice being taken in this calculation of supplements paid in certain minimum-stipend charges.

(2) The same fee to be paid to any one of those authorised to conduct services (see above). When supply is given by a minister of another denomination only 75 per cent of the fee is to be paid, and in all other cases the fee is to be £10.

(3) When the minister of a charge provides supply without requiring to fill his own pulpit, no fee is to be paid, but he may receive an honorarium of £10.

(4) The same fee is payable no matter how many

services are involved. 'If the preacher is not prepared to conduct all the services for which he or she has been engaged, the fee shall be shared equally between or among them.'

(5) Travelling expenses necessarily incurred are to be refunded—bus fare, rail (second class) fare, steamer cabin fare. Where public conveyance is not conveniently available the use of a private car is to be paid for at the lowest rate applicable in the case of a minister—at the time of writing 12p per mile. This was changed from highest to lowest in 1985. In exceptional circumstances, where it has been agreed in advance, the cost of hiring is met.

(6) Weekend board may be reclaimed to a maximum of £20 on production of receipts, but the hope is expressed that wherever possible this will be provided voluntarily or at reduced cost.

Fees and expenses are to be paid before the 'supplier' leaves on the Sunday, and it is most important that this rule should be scrupulously observed. In the case of a vacancy an arrangement may be come to whereby the Treasurer is supplied with vouchers one of which he gives to the person supplying, and the latter forwards this for settlement to the Secretaries of the Department of Ministry and Mission.

Unqualified Persons—The employment for the conduct of public worship of any person other than those listed above is prohibited. Any minister, interim moderator, or sesion clerk engaging the services of such a person is to intimate accordingly to the Presbytery Clerk within 14 days, giving full particulars and stating whether, before engaging the said person, he had made application to one of the Agents. A careful reading of the regulations governing pulpit supply fees would seem to indicate that the proper fee in such a case is £10.

Cost of Supply During Vacancy—Assistance is available from the Maintenance of the Ministry Fund towards meeting the cost of pulpit supply during a vacancy, the charge being borne jointly by the Fund and by the congregation in the proportion that applied to stipend during the last year of the incumbency. When the stipend is paid wholly, or near wholly, from the Fund and local resources are limited, a supply of weekly vouchers may be obtained on giving an undertaking to remit the required contribution throughout the vacancy. A voucher is given to the preacher and remitted by him to the Secretaries (see above).

Supply by Readers

A reader is a member, male or female, of the Church who has been trained and set apart to conduct public worship, which may be done anywhere in the Church. Each Presbytery maintains a List of Readers within its bounds, and a full list is kept by the Probationers and Transference and Admission of Ministers Committee, and this is printed in the Year Book.

The Office of Reader—This is an office of very ancient origin in the Church of Scotland. The Reformed Church in its early stages was inevitably desperately short of qualified ministers, because from the outset it was insistent on the necessity of its ministry being fully equipped academically, so that the many priests who came over had to undergo considerable educational training before being accepted as fit to minister in parishes. This temporary dearth of ministers was met by the employment in many parishes of Readers, a number of whom functioned under the direction of a Superintendent—a system not unlike that of the Methodist circuit. In time the qualified ministers were forthcoming and the Office of Reader lapsed. It was significantly revived after the First World War, again in a time of acute ministerial shortage, and again it lapsed when a regular flow of students became available. The Office was revived in 1958 and is presently governed by the provisions of Act XXVIII of 1974 as amended by Act XXIV of 1978.

Selection—Any member of the Church of Scotland may apply to his Presbytery to be taken in training as a Reader. He should enclose evidence of commendation in the form of a letter from his minister, and an extract Minute from his Kirk Session. The Presbytery, having considered the application and met the applicant and being satisfied as to his suitability, refers the application to the Education Department of the General Assembly where it is dealt with by the Committee on Adult Education.

Training—The course of training is one of guided study, extending normally over two years, and it includes experience of conducting public worship, attendance at one weekend conference, and six months attachment to a congregation (which will not be the candidate's own). Further, a tutor or tutors (not his own minister) appointed by the Presbytery is—or are—to supervise his training. Details of the course are fully set forth in the 1978 Act. On the candidate having satisfactorily concluded his course, the Assembly Committee will furnish the Presbytery with a Certificate of Satisfactory Completion of the Training Course for Readers for presentation to the candidate. In certain circumstances a candidate may be exempted from some part of the course, and in that case the certificate will be appropriately amended. During the period of his training the candidate is not authorised to conduct public worship.

Admission—It is now for the Presbytery to arrange for the admission of the reader, and this will normally, although not necessarily, take place at an ordinary meeting of the court. After the reading of the Preamble the prescribed questions are put (with the phrase 'to discharge the duties of reader' taking the place of 'to discharge the duties of your ministry') and the candidate signs the Formula. He is then set apart in prayer and welcomed as a Reader of the Church with authority to conduct public worship anywhere within the Church. His name is entered on the Roll of Readers of the Presbytery and his name is forwarded to the Probationers' Committee and to the Editor of the Year Book.

Supervision—Readers function under authority of the Presbytery with which they are enrolled, and on leaving the bounds of that Presbytery the Reader should apply for a certificate which he will lodge with the Clerk of the Presbytery within whose bounds he has gone to reside—this is the certificate testifying to status and character. Readers are required at least once every two years to attend an in-service conference approved by the Department of Education. At his own request a

Reader may have his name taken from the Active List without affecting his status as a Reader.

As far as life and doctrine are concerned, it is my opinion that the Reader, like any other layman, is answerable to his own Kirk Session. Were it to be averred that he was preaching heretical doctrines, it would be for the Presbytery to conduct an enquiry into the facts, to instruct him if he were in error, but if he proved obdurate to order the removal of his name from the Roll; but as far as any disciplinary censure was concerned the matter would have to be referred to the Kirk Session.

Availability—The obvious weakness of the system at the present time lies in the fact that the supply of readers is most plentiful in the populous districts where the demand is at its lowest, whereas in the remote areas, where their services would be invaluable, the readers are very thin on the ground. It is difficult to see how this situation can be remedied. In my own experience in Glasgow we were at one time beset by complaints from readers that they had been at great pains to equip themselves for a function which they were rarely if ever given the opportunity to perform. The suggestion was made that their services might be profitably employed on a part-time basis not in the pulpits but in the pastoral work of the Presbytery's parishes, but for this there seemed little enthusiasm. On the other hand it has to be said that an experiment in appointing a team of three readers to supply, under the direction of the Interim Moderator, the needs of a congregation suffering a protracted vacancy, proved reasonably satisfactory, even if it has not been repeated.

Assistants

Ministerial assistance can take quite a variety of different forms—there is the attached student, the student assistant, the ordained assistant, the associate minister, the auxiliary minister, and increasingly a situation is developing where an arrangement is made with a retired minister to render part-time service. There is also the Community Minister.

Student Attachment

It is a prescribed and important part of the preparation for the ministry that a candidate has to engage in a certain amount of practical work concomitantly with the pursuit of his academic studies (*p* 29), and this is achieved by his being attached, during his years at Divinity Faculty, to a series of parishes as determined by the local Liaison Committee. The 1970 regulations governing such attachments provide that they are to operate only in winter and spring terms with no obligations over the Christmas and Easter vacations, that the student is to conduct at least two (preferably three) complete services, that he participate in one (not always the same) Sunday activity, that on most Sundays he assist the minister by taking different parts of the principal service, that he spend not more than one afternoon or evening (three hours) per week in the work of the attachment, and that, while no salary will be paid, expenses necessarily incurred will be refunded by the Committee. Each student is to undertake three attachments during his course—in a different parish each year progressively involving increasing responsibility. The extent of the service is determined by the Committee which also evaluates its success. The Liaison Committee may in certain circumstances arrange a summer attachment of from 12 to 15 weeks in duration, but with a greater degree of midweek participation than a normal term-time attachment, and such an arrangement may be accepted as one of the attachments.

Clearly this exercise is student-orientated, its object being to provide the student with an insight at close quarters into the work of the parish ministry, and any measure of assistance which the minister is likely to gain is purely coincidental and likely in any case to be offset by the burden of guiding and supervising which the system imposes.

Student Assistant

Student assistantships were at one time a regular and, from the students' point of view, a highly popular feature of the training for the ministry. At any time during his university course, and particularly in its final stages, a student might be expected to be engaged as an Assistant in some busy congregation, and in days before the payment of Student Grants the (generally modest) sum paid by way of salary could be a most welcome addition to the student exchequer, and probably went some way to explain the anxiety to achieve a placing. In 1969 this system was brought to an end in terms of a deliverance of the General Assembly, it being thought that the attachment system provided a better form of training.

The following year a petition was presented to the Assembly by the Divinity Students' Council of

Trinity College, Glasgow, asking that Student Assistantships be reintroduced as an optional alternative to student attachments. The Assembly provisionally granted the crave and remitted to the Committee to examine the whole field afresh. The researches of the Committee disclosed that in the other three centres there was a preference for attachments, but that it was generally felt that an option should be available. The position today is that the normal form of practical training is the student attachment, but all four Liaison Committees are free to appoint to student assistantships students who in their opinion would benefit from this form of training. There are not many instances of such assistantships today, although interest appears to be growing.

Probationer Assistant
Almost without exception students, once licensed, are required to serve a Probationary Period (of from eight months to a year) at the direction and under the surveillance of the Committee on Education for the Ministry (*p* 41). A proposal that the period be extended to two years was welcomed, but in 1983 it was abandoned on the grounds of the expense entailed.

Direction—Each Presbytery is required to submit annually a list of those charges within its bounds wherein it is believed a probationer could acquire valuable experience and receive helpful direction and training. In some cases it will be possible for such a congregation itself to meet the cost of salary and expenses, in other cases to make some contribution towards it, while in other cases any contribution at all will be beyond the resources of the local people. The dominant question in the allocation of probationers will always be the possibilities of experience and training and not the financial considerations.

Auxiliary Probationers–Those in training for the Auxiliary Ministry also—on being licensed—have, unless in very exceptional circumstances, to serve a Probationary Period, and this they will do in exactly the same way as students for the regular ministry, except that they will be available for only a limited number of hours (ten perhaps) per week, and that they will not be in receipt of any salary, although they may recover out-of-pocket expenses.

Salary and Expenses–Regulations governing payment of salary and expenses of probationers were approved by the Assembly of 1974 and have from time to time been adjusted since. Today's position is set forth fully on page 43.

Commitment–The Probationary Period may commence any time after licence, but it usually begins not later than the opening of the session's activities at the beginning of September. The probationer is required to give his full time and energy to the work of the assistantship, and while, naturally, this will involve him in study, he is specifically prohibited from any formal matriculation in a University post-graduate course, whether on a part-time or a full-time basis. He acts under the direction and control of the minister, and if the appointment has involved moving into the bounds of a new Presbytery, he has to lodge a certificate with the Clerk and he now comes under the supervision of that Presbytery. An admirable recent innovation is that Presbyteries are officially informed of appointments made within their bounds. In any matter of life or doctrine it is to the Presbytery that he is answerable.

Period of Service—When it comes round to March both probationer and supervising minister send reports to the Committee on Education for the Ministry which decides in light of these whether the period should be sustained. If the appointment has begun on or before 1 September, the period ends on 30 April following. Where the assistant-ship has begun at any other time, it continues for at least eight months. If the periods of practical training referred to above (*p* 170) have not been completed or, (as occasionally happens) have not been completed to the satisfaction of the Committee, the period of compulsory training may be extended, as determined by the Committee. It is not unknown for a probationer to elect to continue for a further year in his assistantship, and in that case it is probable that application will be made for him to be ordained (but see hereunder).

Ordained Assistant

His Probationary Period having been completed to the satisfaction of all concerned, the probationer may, instead of proceeding immediately to look for a charge, elect to serve for a further period as an Assistant, either in the congregation where he has been for the past year, or in some other congregation, and in such a case it is usual that he should be ordained both to allow his rendering of a fuller service and to give him a deeper and more comprehensive experience.

Request for Ordination—The request for the ordination of an Assistant should be directed to the Presbytery by the minister and Kirk Session of the congregation where his service is to be given, and the request should indicate that the probationer has satisfactorily completed his year and has given an undertaking to continue in the position for at least a year after ordination. In considering the request, the Presbytery is enjoined to bear in mind that ordination should be granted to licentiates for very good reasons (either because of the size of the congregation in which they serve or because of the amount of pastoral or parochial work involved)— although I imagine only some very cogent reason would today lead to refusal.

Service of Ordination—This is exactly as it would be for a probationer going to his first charge, and an edict in common form has to be served. Since 1970 ordination as an Assistant has carried with it the right to a seat in Presbytery and Synod.

Conditions—The same conditions apply in regard to salary and expenses as outlined above in the case of probationers, except that the salary is at the rate of 80 per cent of the Minimum Stipend prevailing during the year when ordination is conferred. In this case these figures represent minima and better terms can be given as long as the congregation is meeting all its financial commitments. Generally the arrangement may be terminated (after the promised year) by one month's notice on either side.

While the foregoing represents the law on the subject, the *de facto* position is that scarcely any congregation can afford to maintain an Ordained

Assistant. The increase in salary is only five per cent of the Minimum, but immediately on ordination the appointment attracts the 20 per cent of salary Aged and Infirm Ministers' Fund levy, and as soon as the Probationary Period has been sustained there can be no contribution made from central funds. Today the cost of employing an Ordained Assistant is at best formidable and in most cases prohibitive.

Associate Minister

This is a creation of fairly recent times and there is little law applying to it. It may seem to bear some resemblance to the collegiate ministry which for a long time was the cause of dispeace and misery in parishes afflicted with it. It avoids, however, the two fatal weaknesses of that old system—that two men of perfectly complete status were in charge of a congregation, and that neither had any voice in the choosing of the other. Under the Associate Ministry principle, the minister of the parish is in charge and officially, if not actually, lays down the law, and as minister he has his say in the selection of the man who is to be working with him in so intimate a fashion.

Creation—It is for the Presbytery to determine when an Associate Ministry should be created in a charge. When so deciding, the Presbytery is expected also to define with some precision what are to be the duties of such a ministry, and this it is to do in conference with the minister and Kirk Session of the charge concerned. Normally an Associate Ministry will be created for one of two reasons—either (a) a charge, perhaps because of readjustment, has become of such a size as to demand the services of a second minister, or (b) because there is in the parish an area of special character sufficient to demand a minister freed from other parish responsibilities to look after it. In the former case, care must be taken by the Presbytery in framing the job-specification to ensure that the Associate, while ultimately under the direction of the minister, is given scope for the fulfilment of his own personal ministry and is not seen simply as an Assistant with a blown-up title. In the latter case, the danger is the potential over-departmentalising of the work of two men who should be seen as sharing one common ministry. And in both cases it should be borne in mind that the idea of the Associate Ministry is still in its infancy and that a fair measure of freedom must be allowed to discover how the arrangement can be employed to best advantage.

Tenure—The length of tenure has to be stipulated in the agreement reached when the appointment is made, and a copy of the whole terms is supplied to the appointee before his final acceptance. It should be kept in mind that the achievement of some degree of continuity is one of the principal reasons for having an Associate rather than an Assistant and that the contract should therefore be for a fairly long period. There is nothing to prevent it from being for, say, five years in the first instance with the option of renewal thereafter. On the whole I think this is much to be preferred to the idea of 'ten years with a break for review at the end of five'. When a period is stipulated I imagine the congregation is bound and

I think the Associate should feel equally bound, although a situation could arise which no-one would want to continue for longer than necessary. During the period of his service the Associate will be a member of the Kirk Session but will not act as its Moderator. He will also enjoy a seat in Presbytery and Synod.

Introduction—The Associate, who will have been chosen by the Kirk Session with the concurrence of the minister (ratified, if the Kirk Session so wish, by the congregation itself), has his appointment confirmed by the Presbytery which has to satisfy itself as to his status and credentials, and is introduced to the congregation at an appropriate service. Edictal intimation is not required unless ordination is also involved. Obviously since he will be working in such close fellowship with the minister the latter's concurrence in the choice is of paramount importance.

Payment—The stipend of an Associate Minister will be the subject of a Vacancy Schedule, the amount being determined by the employing congregation in conference with the Presbytery and with concurrence of the Assembly's Committee. He will be provided with a manse or manse allowance in lieu, as well as being paid the usual Listed Expenses, and the Aged and Infirm levy will also be payable. In certain circumstances the Unions and Readjustments Committee may be prepared to recognise the Associate Ministry as a 'New Form of Parish Ministry' and to take over in part or in whole the payment of stipend—but any such agreement must be reached in advance of any steps being taken towards an appointment.

Auxiliary Minister

Full particulars regarding the selection, training, and employment of Auxiliary Ministers will be found on page 59 *ff.*

Assignment–'Auxiliary Ministers may be allotted to such assignments as the Presbytery of the bounds may from time to time determine.' Such assignments may be expected to vary quite considerably in character. In some cases relief to the over-worked minister in an area of deprivation can be in view, or help to a minister in a multi-parish linking, or provision to cover a continued, or at least continuing, vacancy. Whatever the circumstances, the Auxiliary in discharging the duties of his assignment is subject to the oversight of a minister or ministers appointed by the Presbytery of the bounds.

Conditions of Service–These are to be determined by the Presbytery in consultation with the minister of the parish within which the assignment is to operate and are to include a definition of the minimum number of hours per week and the number of weeks per year to be devoted by the Auxiliary, arrangements for the reimbursement of expenses (which will include travelling up to a maximum of 4500 miles per year), and the payment of pulpit supply fees which, however, are not to be exigible in respect of the pulpit of the parish to which he is assigned (*p* 66). A list of 'Proposed Conditions for the Assignment of an Auxiliary Minister' was approved by the Assembly of 1985 (*p* 67).

Duration of Assignment–It is specified in the Act that initially the duration of each assignment is not to exceed five years. Surprisingly the Act goes on to say that 'the Presbytery shall be entitled at any time ... to suspend or terminate the assignment, to renew it up to another five years, or to vary its terms'. It would appear that the contract of service is of a very elastic nature if the Presbytery is to be able at its own hand to vary its terms in so drastic a fashion. It is reasonable to conclude that the Auxiliary will also enjoy some freedom in the matter.

Relation to Courts—During the period of his assignment the Auxiliary is a member of Presbytery and Synod and is eligible to be elected a commissioner to the General Assembly. During the same period he is to be associated with, although not a member of, the Kirk Session; and while the minister or Interim Moderator may authorise him to preside over a meeting of Kirk Session, he can do so only on the very restricted terms applicable to any other moderator *pro tempore*. It would seem that during any period of 'unemployment' the Auxiliary cannot be a member of any court of the Church since his right to sit as a minister is dependent on his holding an assignment, and as long as he remains a minister he cannot sit in the courts as an elder.

Retired Minister

A practice which is spreading fairly rapidly, at least in the cities, and which in light of the cost of probationer assistance is likely to spread further, is that a minister who has resigned from his parish on grounds of age accepts appointment as a part-time assistant in some busy charge with a view principally to lightening the minister's load of pastoral attention, especially perhaps keeping in touch with the house-bound. This is a local and domestic arrangement where agreement is reached by the minister and Kirk Session and the retired minister regarding duties, remuneration, *etc.* The retired minister holds his seat in Presbytery in virtue of being the retired minister of X, not of being Ordained assistant minister at Y. He may be invited to be an Associate Member of Kirk Session but has no vote in it, nor does he function as Moderator unless authorised to act *pro tempore* under the limitations which that involves.

Locum Tenens–A retired minister may be employed as a *locum tenens* in a parish during a time of vacancy. Again this is a domestic arrangement requiring outside approval only in one of two events. First, it is possible that the Presbytery will not approve of the Interim Moderator (being a retired minister) accepting office as locum—a difficulty easily overcome by the appointment of another Interim Moderator. (When delicate re-adjustment negotiations are involved, this dual role can lead to complications better avoided.) Second, when some part of the vacancy expenses are being met out of Maintenance of the Ministry Funds, the approval of that Committee is a *sine qua non* of any financial arrangement with the locum.

There is no rule governing the salary of a locum—it is all a matter of arrangement and will depend to a large extent upon what is to be given by way of service. This may vary from pulpit supply with conduct of funerals and urgent sick visiting, to what amounts to the full work of a settled ministry, and the emoluments have to be adjusted to match.

Community Minister

The story of the origin of this new office makes curious reading. In 1971, arising out of the report of the Special Commission on Priorities in Mission, the Advisory Board was instructed 'to take up the question of what area might most suitably be named as an area organisational experiment of the kind suggested in the report, to consider the possibility of the appointment of an "Enabler", and to bring forward specific proposals to the next General Assembly'. The following year, in pursuance of this, it was reported by the Advisory Board that Drumchapel had, with the approval of the Presbytery of Dumbarton, been chosen as the area, but that the question of the appointment of an 'Enabler' was still under consideration, the functions of such a person not having been very clearly defined in the original report. They went on to promise that this would receive the most careful attention. The following year the Board was happy to report that the appointment had been made of a 'Community Minister' but said not a word in fulfilment of its promise to define duties or responsibilities. The matter now moved into the field of the Home Board who were financing the venture.

In 1974 the latter body reported to the Assembly on what was being done at Drumchapel where, it was said, the work of the Community Minister 'covered many aspects of the life of the community, such as participation in the activities of the community, helping to set up a newspaper, promoting amenities, supporting self-help groups, arranging parties for deprived children and coordinating distribution of gifts at Christmas; seeking to formulate answers to the real needs of the people of the area. A close relationship is kept up with all the congregational agencies in the locality'. It was added that his duties had also included the promotion of ecumenical understanding and Christian action, the establishment of house-Churches, and keeping in touch with congregations in the area.

Responsibility for the experiment next passed from the Home Board to the Maintenance of the Ministry Committee, and from them to the Unions and Readjustments Committee under the umbrella of 'New Forms of Parish Ministry'. As far as I am aware no statement has yet been before the Assembly of the precise duties of a Community Minister. In 1985 there were nine Community Ministers employed within the Church. While, to mix metaphors, one would not want to see an experiment laced up in a strait-jacket, I am satisfied that advantage would accrue from a little more specification in this field.

Appointment—It will be only indirectly that any one parish minister in particular will benefit from the setting up of a Community Ministry in his area, and so the initiative in this field must lie with the Presbytery which has to make approach to the Unions and Readjustments Committee. If it is agreed in principle that such a project should proceed, consultation will take place regarding the area to be served and the nature of the work to be undertaken, and the appointment will be made by the Committee in consultation with the Presbytery. For the discharge of his duties the Community

Minister is answerable to the Committee; for life
and doctrine he comes under the jurisdiction of
the Presbytery.

Lay Missionaries

The Lay Missionary is an agent of the Parish
Assistance Committee appointed to preach and
exercise pastoral care under the direction of a
minister and Kirk Session. Such missionaries are
generally employed in two entirely different situations: first in the more remote corners of the
country where the missionary may be almost
wholly responsible for a particular area within a
very large parish, probably having a Mission
Church there; and second in the cities, where the
missionary is appointed to assist the minister with
the pastoral work in a very difficult and demanding area, again probably functioning from mission
premises. Lay Missionaries are entitled to preach,
in many cases doing so practically every Sunday,
but not being ordained they cannot dispense the
sacraments. From time to time it has been suggested that advantage would result from the
ordination of missionaries, particularly in a situation where they are working in lonely isolated
corners of the earth or on islands which the parish
minister can visit only rarely. The Assembly,
however, has steadfastly set its face against this,
although the question will doubtless arise again as
the number of Auxiliary Ministers increases. In a
limited number of cases where a Lay Missionary is
alone on an island it has been agreed with the
Registrar General that permission be given to

conduct marriages according to the forms of the Church of Scotland. Although the right to marry has always been confined to the ordained ministry there is no reason on theological grounds for such restriction.

Candidature–A candidate must be a man of strong Christian character and conviction and a member of the Church of Scotland, and his candidature has to be approved by his Presbytery of residence. The Parish Assistance Committee arranges for him a suitable course of study. He serves one probationary year in a post to which he is directed by the Committee, and after that he is commissioned a Lay Missionary 'by the General Assembly or by such subordinate court as may be named by the General Assembly'—which will normally be the Presbytery.

Appointment–Appointments to parishes are made by the Parish Assistance Committee with concurrence of the minister and Kirk Session of the charge concerned. At the instance of the Committee, the Missionary may at any time be transferred to another parish. On being so transferred he is welcomed at a service in the Parish Church (or the Mission Church as may be appropriate) conducted by the Parish Minister. He retires at the age of 70, although in special circumstances he may be allowed to continue beyond that age.

Relation to Courts–The Missionary if he is an elder may be admitted to the Kirk Session of the charge where he works, and in that case he may be appointed representative elder to the Presbytery. In any case, and whether or not he is an elder, he has the right *ex officio* to sit in Presbytery as a Corresponding Member. If not an elder he may be invited to attend and speak at Session meetings, but without voting powers. When he moves from one Presbytery to another he has to lodge a certificate. For the performance of his duties he is responsible to the Parish Assistance Committee, for life and doctrine he is responsible to his Kirk Session.

Salary—Lay Missionaries are on the pay-roll of the Parish Assistance Committee. In 1986 the basic salary was £6380 with seniority payments of £500 after seven and £750 after 14 years' service. In addition, those serving in Shetland receive a supplement of £250, those in Orkney and the Western Isles receive £150. A house is also provided, failing which a payment of £1000 per annum is made in lieu. A retirement pension at the rate of £1100 per annum is paid to Missionaries who have completed 20 years of service.

Numbers—In 1985 the Parish Assistance Committee reported 27 Lay Missionaries in service, 11 of them in Highland and Island communities.

The Diaconate

Deaconesses and Church Sisters have for a long time been an important feature of the life of the Kirk. In 1962 the General Assembly approved an elaborate 'Scheme for Deaconesses' brought forward by the then Order of Deaconesses which was designed to give (a) more emphasis to the office of Deaconess, (b) a place to Presbytery not only as the court of commissioning but as a court to which a Deaconess is responsible for her life and doctrine,

and (c) more responsibility to the Deaconess
Council. In 1979, on the recommendation of the
Deaconess Board, it was resolved 'that the office of
the Diaconate shall be open to men and women so
that men may be commissioned in a similar way to
that in which women are commissioned at present'.
It was also resolved to substitute 'Diaconate' for
'Deaconess' in all appropriate places. In 1982 the
Scheme (of 1962) was amended, although the only
significant change was the introduction of the
possibility of the office being held by a man. In
1985 as part of the administration-readjustment
being undertaken by the Assembly Council, the
Diaconate Board became the Diaconate Committee
and was embraced among the Associated Committees of the Department of Ministry and Mission.

Definition—A Deacon or Deaconess is described
as 'one who has, under a call from God, pledged
himself or herself to the service of Jesus Christ
and His Church and has been trained and commissioned thereto in conformity with the doctrine
and discipline of the Church of Scotland. It is a
distinctive office agreeable to the Word of God'.

It is emphasised that the office is open to men on
the same terms as women and the 'Scheme' is at
pains to use 'he or she' *etc* throughout. I have in
all of this book, as explained in the Preface, used
the masculine form alone to avoid the dreary
repetition of alternatives and the complicated
constructions that can sometimes result. In this
case the *de facto* position is that at the time of
writing the office is exclusively held by women and
it seems reasonable, therefore, that if only one
gender is to be used it should be the feminine—it
being understood that men are included.

Function–The function of a Deaconess is to exercise a ministry of an evangelistic, pastoral, educational, or social nature in the work of a parish or chaplaincy, or in some other service which, although outside the immediate work of the Church, is approved by the Board with the concurrence of the Presbytery concerned. Of late years there has been an increase in the last-named category of employment. The report of 1962 disclosed that of 89 Deaconesses on the active list, 66 were working in parishes, 18 were working with Assembly Committees and only three were otherwise employed. In 1986 the total had fallen to 58 of whom 37 were in parishes, nine with Committees, and 13 otherwise. (Mathematical purists will be quick to point out that in neither case do the figures add up correctly!)

Candidature–A candidate has to apply to the Diaconate Committee and will be interviewed by that body. If satisfied regarding sense of vocation, fitness and basic background, the Committee may accept the candidate and if so will notify the Presbytery of her residence for its interest. In case of rejection the candidate has a right to petition the Assembly.

Training–Every candidate must satisfy the Committee that she has a knowledge of the Bible, of Christian doctrine, of Church History (particularly Scottish), an understanding of the Church, and is able to relate all these to individual and corporate life today, and that she has practical experience and understanding of Christian education and the communication of the Gospel to different ages and groups. Training is normally taken at St Colm's Education Centre and College. Over and above this, the Deaconess may be expected to take more specialised training prescribed by the Department or Committee for which she is to be working. The Diaconate Committee prescribes a Probationary Period (which may be extended), informing the Presbytery within which it is to be served.

Commissioning – A candidate, having satisfied the requirements in regard to training and probation and being a communicant member of the Church of Scotland and over 21 years of age, may be commissioned, an exercise performed by the Presbytery at a special service held for this purpose. This normally will take place in the church where her work is to be centred and the Presbytery will associate with it in the service those Deaconesses who are in attendance. Having been so commissioned the Deaconess is entitled to append after her name the letters 'DCS' (Deaconess of the Church of Scotland), and to wear the badge and uniform of a Deaconess.

Answerability – For the performance of her service, the Deaconess is answerable to the Department or Committee or secular body which is employing her, but of course if she is working in a parish she will take her day-to-day orders from the minister. In the matter of life and doctrine she is answerable to the Presbytery within whose bounds she is serving; or failing such a Presbytery, she is under the jurisdiction of the Presbytery which commissioned her. She may voluntarily resign her commission, but may be deprived of it only by judgment of the Presbytery, with the usual right of appeal to Synod and General Assembly.

Relation to the Courts—There is nothing to prevent a Deaconess being ordained an elder and being admitted to the Kirk Session of the parish where she is serving. The Assembly of 1958 ruled that Deaconesses working in parishes should be invited to attend Session meetings when matters affecting their work were under discussion, that Deaconesses should be appointed to membership of Presbytery Committees, and that the Nomination Committee should consider their appointment to Assembly Committees on which women serve. The Assembly of 1980 ordained that a Deaconess serving within the bounds should *ex officio* be a Corresponding Member of Presbytery. On moving from the bounds of one Presbytery to those of another, the Deaconess has to take a certificate vouching for her status, life and character.

In most Presbyteries Deaconesses are 'received' at one of their meetings each year and occasion is taken to pay tribute to the service they are rendering.

Salary—Terms and conditions of service are determined by the Department, Committee, or other employing authority. Those in the employ of the Department of Ministry and Mission were in 1986 being paid £6380 per annum and, if no house was provided, an annual sum of £1000 in lieu. Seniority Payments apply—after seven years £500 and after 14 years £700—and also Supplements of £250, when working in Shetland, and £150 in Orkney or the Western Isles. A pension scheme is operated by the Scottish Widows' Fund and Life Assurance whereby Deaconesses pay 1.5 per cent of salary and on retirement receive either a pension or a lump sum (tax-free) and a reduced pension.

Licence to Preach

In 1956 it was agreed by the General Assembly that certain candidates for the Diaconate, having the required qualifications, should receive a course of theological training which would 'fit them to act as Assistants in parishes, Chaplains in Universities and Training Colleges, Teachers of Religious Education in schools and Colleges and similar spheres of service'; and

(1) that such candidates if found suitable by the Deaconess Committee are to be recommended to the Presbytery not only for commissioning but also for licensing as Preachers of the Word, without reference to probation for the Holy Ministry;

(2) that regular preaching and regular participation in the conduct of public worship is to be only by Deaconesses so qualified and licensed; and

(3) that any Deaconess may apply to the Committee on Education for the Ministry to have such additional training prescribed so that she may qualify for such licence.

The decision in 1968 that women should be eligible for ordination as ministers on the same terms as men was bound to render rather superfluous the legislation for Deaconesses to train for licence to preach since in effect this was now equivalent to becoming a Probationer for the Holy Ministry.

It will be noted that the restriction of preaching and conducting public worship to Deaconesses licensed to preach refers to the 'regular' exercise of these functions, which would seem to indicate that all duly commissioned deaconesses are available for occasional pulpit supply, although in the most recent Act (of 1986) they are not included.

8

Other
Appointments

Our grandfathers would have found it unthink-
able that a minister should be other than minister
of a parish, a professor in a school of Divinity, or a
missionary overseas—unless, perhaps, he was a
'stickit minister', in which case, being fully qualified
but having been unable to secure a call, he was
probably eking out a fairly miserable existence
acting as tutor in the household of some wealthy
family. It is only within the last 40 years or so that
there has occurred the wide diversification in the
work of the ministry so that today there are
something like 180 non-parochial posts within the
service of the Church filled by persons with the
status of ordained ministers.

The Kirk has always been chary about encouraging *ministerium vagum* and in consequence has been
reluctant to grant ordination unless to those about
to enter upon a settled charge. As long ago as
1896, however, the Assembly drew the attention of
Presbyteries to the discretionary powers which
might be exercised in granting, under suitable
conditions, ordination to probationers who were of
sufficient experience and who were engaged in
regular service. As a result of this, some probationers were ordained in their parish assistantships
and continued to serve there longer than they

might otherwise have done. At that time the term 'ordained probationer' was not infrequently used to describe such a person, although that obviously is a contradiction in terms and I think is not often heard today. Latterly the principle was established that ordination might be given when the person concerned had already served a year in the assistantship and gave an undertaking to stay for at least another 12 months. Such appointments were not of frequent occurrence and until 1970 they did not carry a seat in Presbytery. Due to financial considerations (*p* 176) they are today of still less frequent occurrence.

One of the features of Church life today is the increasing interest in 'New Forms of Parish Ministry' and there are now a number of appointments within the parish system which involve ordination and which are entitled to a seat in Presbytery—there is the Ordained Assistant, the Associate Minister, and the Community Minister, and these positions are dealt with at length on pages 174, 176 and 182 respectively. For our present purpose let it suffice that in each case the appointee is ordained and introduced after service of an edict in common form and in a Presbytery Service comparable to that for ordination and induction, except, of course, that there is no question to the congregation. The official status of such a person is 'Minister without Charge'.

Apart from these diverse forms of parish ministry there are a number of appointments which are most intimately connected with the witness of the Church but which fall completely outwith the compass of the parish system. It is with these that I hope to deal in some detail in the present chapter.

University Teachers

Before the Union of 1929 students in training for the ministry of the Church of Scotland were taught in the Divinity Faculties of the four universities, while those hoping to enter the United Free Church took their Arts course in the universities but then moved for their Divinity training to one of the three colleges—New College in Edinburgh, Trinity College in Glasgow, and Christ's College in Aberdeen—all of which had been established by the Free Church immediately following upon the Disruption. Each of these institutions carried a complete teaching staff to cover all the disciplines considered necessary for the ministry—the study of the Old and New Testaments, of Systematic Theology and of Church History. As a result of the Union of 1929, Faculty and College came together and the staffs were merged, although the chairs were still seen as University chairs and Church chairs—and were paid accordingly. By what is now graciously described as 'a process of natural wastage', the duplication gradually disappeared and by filling only the University chairs, the Church was increasingly relieved of its financial responsibility in the matter of salaries. Another change that not unnaturally took place was that the University Courts felt increasingly free to appoint to teaching posts in the Divinity Faculties staff other than Church of Scotland ministers, so that at the time of writing the point has been reached where, out of a total of 58 teaching posts, 34 are filled by ministers of the Church of Scotland, 21 by those attached to other denominations and three by licentiates of the Church of Scotland.

In the case where a licentiate of the Church of Scotland is appointed to a chair, lectureship or readership in a Divinity Faculty, the Presbytery will normally be prepared to ordain him to the ministry and will do so as soon as conveniently possible after he takes up office, normally at a Service held in the Chapel of the University where he teaches. It may be—and it sometimes happens —that the person appointed elects not to be ordained and in that case, of course, he retains his status as a licentiate.

Board of Nomination to Church Chairs—A concordat has been reached between Church and University with regard to appointments to chairs and senior posts within the Faculties of Divinity. Six persons are appointed by the University and the same number by the Assembly, and these constitute a Board for making nominations to fill such vacancies. In terms of the Universities (Scotland) Acts of 1932 and 1966, if this Board brings forward a nomination carrying the support of two-thirds of its entire numerical strength the person so nominated will automatically be appointed by the University Court. He will hold his office at the pleasure of that same University Court, and there is nothing the Church, were it so minded, could do to unseat him.

Who May Be Appointed—Time was when appointees to teaching posts in the Divinity Faculties were drawn exclusively from the ranks of the parish

ministry, often men who had given years in that
service. In this respect things have completely
changed, and that, I imagine, for two reasons. For
one thing, our relentless pursuit of readjustment
has now ensured that there are not many—if there
are any—charges where it is still possible for a man
faithfully to carry through the work of his parish
and yet find time for the additional study required
to equip him for a teaching post. And for another,
the University pattern is altering, particularly in
the light of recent cut-backs in University staffing,
so that he who aspires to follow an academic career
will be at pains to secure for himself, right from the
outset, a posting, however modest, within the
academic world, being convinced that if he moves
out of that world, he will not find it easy to get back
in again. Exactly what effect this change is going to
have on the character of the teaching is an
interesting question which only time will answer.

College Principal—While in respect of most affairs
concerned with equipping students for the work of
the ministry the Faculties have taken over from the
Church Colleges, the latter bodies continue to
function in many matters of particular interest to
Church of Scotland students, and each has a
Principal appointed by the General Assembly and
functioning quite apart from the Dean of the
Faculty. In the case of all such appointments,
a Service of Introduction is arranged by the
Presbytery within whose bounds the Principal
teaches and he is required to answer the prescribed
questions and to sign the Formula. Since in a case
of this kind the appointment lies within the power
and discretion of the Church, any refusal to

subscribe could have serious consequences as far as the appointment was concerned.

Courts of the Church—Under the earliest Presbyterian set-up only the Professor of Divinity was *ex officio* a member of Presbytery, but on the other hand each University had the right to appoint a commissioner to the General Assembly. Today any minister of the Church of Scotland holding a teaching post in a Faculty of Divinity in Scotland is secured a seat in Presbytery in terms of the 1970 Act, and while originally this meant the Presbytery within whose bounds his University was situated, he may now elect to sit in the Presbytery of his place of residence. The right to a seat continues after retirement on grounds of age or ill health.

When a minister is appointed to such a post he is expected to lodge with the appropriate Presbytery Clerk a certificate from the Presbytery of his former charge or teaching post, and when this is done the Presbytery will arrange for him to be received into its membership on affirming that he adheres to the vows of his ordination and on his signing the Formula. It must be clearly recognised that the signing of the Formula is a test not for the chair in the University but for the seat in the Presbytery.

Colleges of Education

The Scottish Colleges of Education make appointments of ministers—generally of the Church of Scotland—to be Lecturers and Principal Lecturers in Religious Education. Such appointments are made by, and are held at the will of, the College without any reference to the Church. The appointees are entitled to sit in Presbytery on re-affirming their ordination vows and signing the Formula; and on retirement, for age or health, they retain their seats. It is worthy of note that in terms of the Act anent Membership of Presbytery (1970, revised 1986) this refers exclusively to Scottish Colleges of Education.

The identical considerations (including the reservation about 'Scottish') apply to Lecturers in Biblical Studies in Scottish Universities.

Overseas Appointments

The overseas work of the Church is today under the direction of the Board of World Mission and Unity, a body created in 1984 to weld into one Department that which had been the Overseas Council and the Committee on Inter-Church Relations. The Overseas Council in turn represented the union effected in 1964 of what had originally been four separate and distinct spheres of enterprise—the work done in the Continental (and what used to be the Colonial) charges, work among the Jews, and what was for so long enthusiastically supported as 'Foreign Missions'. Today there are three branches of the work of the Board and they might respectively be called 'Expatriate Ministries', 'Work Among Jewish People' and 'Missionaries Overseas'.

Expatriate Ministries
The full title of this branch of the work of the Board is 'Ministry to English-Speaking Reformed

Congregations Overseas' and that is a good enough working definition of what it is all about. The Scot being the kind of gregarious animal which history has shown him to be, it was inevitable that from early days congregations of expatriate Scots should have formed themselves in many cities of Europe. At one time there were as many as 11 Scottish congregations in Holland alone. Some of the European charges go back to the 17th century. It is interesting to recall that during the days of intense persecution under the Stuarts when Presbyterian ordination constituted a criminal offence, many Scots ministers (of whom James Renwick was one) were ordained in our Kirk in Rotterdam. The same kind of considerations later applied wherever Scots in any great numbers were found in our colonial outposts. Due largely to such accidents of history, the Church of Scotland maintains a presence in 11 cities of Europe, in parts of South America and the Carribean, as well as in Sri Lanka. These charges are no longer—if they ever were— exclusively Scottish but have become both international and interdenominational. They are, however, bound by a common use of the English language and by a common adherence to the Reformed tradition.

Constitutional Position—The precise form of government to which these congregations are subject differs from one case to another—and in every case to the standard Scottish pattern! Sometimes, as in Holland, there is a direct link with the courts of the national Church. Ministers are appointed by the Board after consultation with local parties, and appointments are for a fixed period of years, although this may in the event be extended. The European charges are bound into a Presbytery which acts as a very important meeting-place for ministers and for congregational repre-sentatives alike, as well as providing a direct line of access to the General Assembly without interven-tion of the Board. The Presbytery has somewhat restricted powers as conferred in terms of the Act of 1978 that had replaced earlier legislation. The Presbytery is given 'similar powers and functions and similar membership to Presbyteries in Scotland' but subject always to the peculiar circumstances obtaining in the local set-up (for example, that the body corresponding to the Kirk Session may be known by another name and may differ consider-ably from a Kirk Session in powers and functions) and to the fact that ministers are appointed by the Board which is also responsible for oversight of their work. The Presbytery of Europe is included for the issue of all material that goes down for discussion and comment, including Overtures under the Barrier Act. Clearly, of course, the Presbytery differs from a home Presbytery in that it has no 'bounds', being just a collection of scattered congregations, and in that it has no standing vis-à-vis the State.

Appointment—As has been said, appointments to all of these charges are made by the Board, and any minister interested in this kind of work would do well to make his interest known to the respon-sible member of the secretariat of the Board. Vacancies are normally advertised and applica-tions invited from ministers interested.

Work Among Jewish People

From very early days the Kirk has had a peculiar concern for the Jewish people, and that concern today expresses itself in such activities as the running of the Tabeetha School in Jaffa (a school which draws pupils—boys and girls—from every nationality), in the provision of a Church and Hospice at Tiberias in Galilee, in the running of the Scots Memorial Church and Hospice of St Andrew at Jerusalem (a memorial to the many Scots men who died fighting under Allenby in Palestine in the First World War), in work in Budapest, and in support of a wide variety of local ventures nearer home. At least two Church of Scotland ministers are permanently engaged in this work in Israel, being centred in Jerusalem and at Tiberias, in each of which there is a congregation of local people and to which tourists are attracted in large numbers. The ministers are appointed by and are answerable to the Board— but see hereunder.

Presbytery of Jerusalem—This Presbytery now functions in terms of an Act of 1979. It is specifically given 'power to licence and power to ordain medical and other lay missionaries when required to do so by the Board of World Mission and Unity'. It appoints two commissioners—a minister and an elder—to each General Assembly', and while it does not have the right to make returns to Barrier Act Overtures, it 'may receive such Overtures and all other documents sent down to Presbyteries for discussion and comment, and may transmit comment to the General Assembly'. Although it has no standing in the appointment of ministers and missionaries it is specifically declared 'that a missionary appointed by the Overseas Council shall remain under the jurisdiction and discipline of the Presbytery'. Considering the highly intimate nature of such a Presbytery and how restricted its numbers are, it is difficult to see how it could effectively exercise discipline over its own membership. It is a very small Presbytery indeed, performing very limited functions, and it has been continued thus largely in response to a plea that such status greatly strengthens the hands of those who are working in the field, particularly vis-à-vis the departments of government.

Missionaries Overseas

The whole conception of the Church's commitment in the developing countries has altered very radically from the day when we sent out 'missionaries to convert the heathen'. For one thing, these developing countries now have their own well-established, independent, indigenous Churches, and our efforts must consist in trying to get alongside to collaborate with them, functioning within their structures, and learning from them no less than teaching them. And for another thing, the situation has now developed where the phrase 'working among the heathen' has assumed a new meaning—every parish minister is doing just that. A further radical change lies in the fact that while for an earlier generation foreign missionary work was seen as the commitment of a lifetime, today we are happy that ministers and others should give a limited spell of service in the overseas field before returning to take up a home charge.

Appointment—Missionaries nowadays serve as doctors, teachers, social workers, nurses, accountants and in a variety of other ways no less than as ministers. They also assist in theological training in colleges. Emphasis is placed on the two-way nature of the traffic so that mission at home is enriched by visits from overseas Christians. Lists of vacancies are published regularly and enquiries about possible opportunities of service should be addressed to the Deputy General Secretary at 121 George Street.

Constitutional Position—In a day when the Church was extensively committed in the missionary field, that work was organised on a Presbyterial basis with congregations grouped in Presbyteries bearing such unlikely names as Bengal, Rajputana, The Gold Coast, Livingstonia, Jamaica or Jerusalem. Twenty-five years ago there were no fewer than 16 such Presbyteries. With the changes in the character of our work and the emergence of strong local Churches (sometimes the outcome of ecumenical coming together) these courts have lost whatever relevance they ever possessed, so that by 1964 all (except Jerusalem) had disappeared and ministers are now members of the courts of the newly created Churches and subject to their jurisdiction and control. In the case where there is no such affiliation, a minister continues to be a member of the home Presbytery from which he went, or of that which ordained him, as the case may be. Missionaries at home on furlough, being ministers or elders ordained under the home Formula, or licentiates of our own who have been ordained overseas, provided they hold a certificate from the

Board of World Mission and Unity, have a right to a place at the General Assembly as Corresponding Members. Ministers working overseas in this way are, on their return, entitled to a Certificate of Eligibility (*p* 54 *ff*) which will allow them to be nominated in vacancies; or, if they have retired on the grounds of age or for reasons of health, then on taking up permanent residence in Scotland or England they have a right to a seat in the Presbytery within whose bounds they reside.

Chaplains to Her Majesty's Forces

Each year in its report to the General Assembly the Committee on chaplains to Her Majesty's Forces issues an appeal for young ministers to offer their services 'for this challenging and rewarding type of ministry'. This ministry of the Church is exercised in a very special environment since a great deal of it is furth of Scotland and all of it in situations and under pressures peculiar to service life. It should also be noted that much of it is concerned not only with servicemen but also with their wives and children, far from home, with all the complications that this implies. It is, therefore, not surprising to read that in 1985 no fewer than 247 children were baptised by our Chaplains.

Appointment—The method of appointment and the terms and conditions of service vary considerably according to the particular arm of the Services concerned, and anyone interested in responding to the challenge is advised to get in touch with the Honorary Secretary of the Committee, Mr Thomas M Hunter at 42 Melville Street, Edinburgh.

Royal Navy—In the Royal Navy, the Church of Scotland and the English Free Churches form one administrative unit under the direction of a Principal Chaplain appointed by the Board of Admiralty on the advice of the Advisory Council on Naval Chaplaincies Services. A candidate for a naval chaplaincy (who must be prepared to serve ashore or afloat in any part of the world) is recommended by our Committee on Chaplains to HM Forces to the Principal Chaplain who then nominates him to the Admiralty. Appointments are in the first instance for four years, after which a 16 year pensionable commission may be offered, and in certain circumstances this may be extended until the chaplain reaches the age of 55. At the time of writing there are six full-time Royal Navy chaplains from the Church of Scotland and one from the Presbyterian Church of Ireland.

Regular Army—Ministers of the Church of Scotland serve within the Royal Army Chaplains' Department. This is a unified organisation comprising Chaplains of the main traditions of the Churches in the United Kingdom, the number of Chaplains allocated to each Church being in proportion to the number of servicemen claiming to belong to these denominations. Appointment of Chaplains is made by the Chaplain General, on behalf of the Secretary of State, of those ministers who are recommended by the Committee on Chaplains to HM Forces. In the first instance they serve for from three to five years, after which by mutual agreement they can either extend their appointment with the possibility of a permanent Commission which allows them to serve to the age of 55 years, or they may return to the civilian ministry. Currently there is an establishment for 21 ministers of the Church of Scotland to serve as Chaplains, four of these appointments being held by ministers of other Presbyterian Churches.

Royal Air Force—The Advisory Board on Chaplaincy Services in the Royal Air Force includes one Church of Scotland representative. Within the Air Force, Presbyterian, Methodist, Baptist and Congregational Churches work as one group, day to day control being in the hands of the Principal Chaplain (PMUB) at headquarters. Appointments to commissions in the Chaplains branch are made by the RAF, but no applicant will be considered who is not approved by his own denomination. The Committee on Chaplains to HM Forces is informed by the Principal Chaplain when vacancies arise in the Church of Scotland ranks so that the Committee may select and nominate suitable candidates. At the time of writing there are ten commissioned chaplains in the RAF as well as two Chaplains Assistants, these being Deaconesses of our Church.

Part-Time Chaplaincies—Appointments are also made of parish ministers as part-time chaplains in the Royal Naval Reserve, the Sea Cadet Corps, the Territorial Army, the Army Cadet Force, the Air Training Corps and also as Officiating Chaplains in all three Services. Since some of these posts carry certain responsibilities in the event of an outbreak of war, appointments to them have to carry the approval of the Presbytery concerned.

Relation to Presbytery—A Chaplain to the Forces is a member of Presbytery: if serving in Scotland it is the Presbytery of the bounds within which he serves, if in England or Europe it is the respective Presbytery, or if elsewhere it is the Presbytery he left to join the Forces or the Presbytery which ordained him for the purpose. A good deal of laxity obtains in the application of these conditions and out of 32 chaplains exactly half are entered as members of the Presbytery of England.

Kirk Sessions—In terms of an act of 1952 a Kirk Session may be formed in a Scottish unit of the Forces. Where it is desired to take advantage of this provision, application is made to the Committee on Chaplains which has to satisfy itself that the application carries the approval of the chaplain concerned, that the numbers are such, and that the prospect of the numbers being maintained are such, as to justify the step. If so satisfied the Committee may authorise the formation of a Kirk Session consisting of the chaplain as Moderator and not less than two duly ordained elders. Once established in this way such a Kirk Session may add to its numbers by a simple resolution so to do. Each such Kirk Session is to be associated with a Presbytery—usually that of the Scottish depot of the unit, failing which the Presbytery of Edinburgh —but this will in no way affect the Presbyterial affiliation of the chaplain as defined in the previous paragraph. It was reported to a recent Assembly that there were five such Sessions functioning in Scottish regiments.

Forces Registers—The General Assembly of 1970 approved legislation whereby the Committee on Chaplains to HM Forces is required to maintain a Register of all persons admitted to full communion during their period of service with the Forces. The Committee is further required to issue to such persons on request on their returning to civilian life, a certificate testifying to this. The Committee also maintains a record of all who have been baptised in the Services, and again a certificate may be obtained on application to the Secretary of the Committee. The Committee complains that they meticulously prepare and maintain these registers but that proper use is not being made of them at the receiving end. The co-operation of parish ministers is sought in ensuring that when a returned Services man or woman attaches to a congregation, the minister concerned will get in touch with the Secretary of the Committee with a view to securing the relevant certificate. During 1985, eight adults were baptised and 28 persons were admitted to full communion in the Forces.

Other Chaplaincies

There are in the Kirk today a variety of other chaplaincies which it may be convenient to deal with under the one heading—these other chaplaincies serve Universities, Hospitals, Industry and Prisons. The first three come under the care and direction of the Chaplains Committee of the Department of Ministry and Mission, while Prison Chaplaincies are the responsibility of the Prison Chaplaincies Board, a body appointed by, and which reports directly to, the General Assembly.

Chaplains to Universities
Each of the four ancient Scottish Universities engages the services of a University Chaplain and

these, so far at least, have invariably been ministers of the Church of Scotland. In Glasgow the appointment is part-time, the Chaplain also being a lecturer in the Faculty of Divinity. The appointment is made by the University authorities who are directly responsible for paying and housing him and for the oversight of his duties. In the case where a licentiate is appointed, the Presbytery of the bounds takes steps to conduct a Service of Ordination, and this will be held in the University Chapel.

In the case of the younger universities of Strathclyde, Stirling and Heriot Watt, a chaplaincy service is provided by the Department of Ministry and Mission in collaboration with the relevant university authority—who are invariably most cooperative. In Stirling the appointment is part-time, the chaplain also being a parish minister. Appointments are made by the Chaplains Committee which is also responsible for salary, housing and expenses, and which, of course, can also have a word to say about how the duties are to be discharged. In every case the Presbytery of the bounds is consulted regarding an appointment. There is at present no chaplaincy at the University of Dundee

In both Edinburgh and Glasgow from time to time the appointment has been made of a Chaplain to Overseas Students. In these two centres this represents an ecumenical exercise supported financially by a group of denominations and under the guidance and control of a local ecumenical committee.

Chaplains to Hospitals

While ministers had always been regular visitors in hospitals, and while there were many instances where a particular minister was recognised as chaplain to a particular institution, visiting through all its wards, arranging regular services, *etc*, it was not until the National Health Service scheme came into operation in 1948 that official appointments were first made of chaplains to hospitals and a system was established whereby they received payment for their services. Mostly these are parish ministers, with an occasional minister of another denomination, and they undertake this as an additional duty. For the purpose of calculating income from all sources for Minimum Stipend purposes, such payments are not included. In some of the larger institutions, full-time appointments are made with the approval of the Regional Health Board. At the time of writing there are 12 ministers engaged full-time as Hospital Chaplains, 11 of them ministers of the Church of Scotland, while the number of part-time chaplains is over 300. The custom is growing of appointing Chaplain's Assistants, mostly women. At present there are five, two of them ordained ministers.

By arrangement with the Department of Health and Social Security the Chaplains Committee of the Department of Ministry and Mission acts as an 'employing authority' in respect of these chaplaincies—that is to say, appointments are made by the Committee (after conference with the Presbytery and with concurrence of the appropriate Health Board) and in due course payment is made by them direct to the chaplains, they in turn being reimbursed by the DHSS (except to the extent that the latter pay only 7.5 per cent of the 20 per cent payable to the Retirement Scheme Committee in respect of the full-time appointees). Where a full-time appointment is to be made, this is the subject of the fullest consultation between the Committee and the Presbytery concerned and also with the relevant Hospital Board.

Chaplains to Industry
Under the direction of the Industrial Mission Organiser chaplains are appointed to serve in a variety of offices, shipyards, factories, *etc*, mainly on a voluntary and part-time basis. There are, however, four Church of Scotland ministers employed full-time as Industrial Chaplains. Full-time appointments are made by the Mission Committee which also provides the stipend, expenses and accommodation (although 15 per cent of costs come from an Industrial Mission Trust which receives donations from industry and from trade unions). Because it is generally accepted that the approach to Industrial Mission must be along ecumenical lines, the central organisation is through a sub-committee of the Mission Committee on which all the major denominations are represented, as are representatives of the Roman Catholic Scottish National Council for the Lay Apostolate, and representatives of local industrial mission activity. Vacancies are advertised and applications considered from ministers of any denomination. Selection is by an interviewing committee with a representation from industry and from the relevant Presbytery. In the case of

the part-time industrial chaplain it is very often the parish minister who is invited to act.

Chaplains to Prisons

Chaplains are appointed to prisons, borstal institutions, detention centres, *etc*, by the Home and Health Department on the recommendation of the Prison Chaplaincies Board which, of course, consults with the Presbytery concerned. At present there is no full-time prison chaplaincy in Scotland.

Integration with Parish Ministry

The considerable increase in the number and variety of chaplaincies in recent times raises problems in connection with the principle that a minister may not perform ministerial functions in the parish of another except with the other's permission or with the authority of the Presbytery. For a variety of reasons, most of them administrative, these appointments are generally made by the Chaplains section of the Mission Committee, which is also responsible, if not for paying, at least for collecting and transmitting the salary. It is, though, essential that every such appointment should have the authority and approval of the Presbytery concerned. For it is only the Presbytery of the bounds which may permit one minister to enter the parish of another for the discharge of such limited ministerial functions (including perhaps administration of the sacraments) as the Presbytery may specifically authorise. The concurrence of the Presbytery in the appointment to the chaplaincy raises a presumption that this degree of authority has been conferred. When the appointment is made by an outside body it is not enough for the Presbytery to 'note' that this has been done. If the minister appointed is a minister of the Church of Scotland, the Presbytery must at the very least be asked to authorise what could otherwise be seen as intrusion into the parish of another.

Confirmation—It is not uncommon that a long-term patient in hospital (to take an example) expresses a desire to enter the full membership of the Church. In such a case the chaplain should get in touch with the patient's own minister, or if there is no Church connection with the minister of the parish of residence, he should arrange to give him a short course of instruction, and should, with the approval of the Kirk Session concerned, admit and receive him, subsequently ensuring that his name has been entered on the appropriate Communion Roll.

Baptism—Where there are urgent or special circumstances rendering necessary the administration of infant baptism within the context of the work of a hospital chaplain, he should so administer and as soon as possible thereafter send particulars to the minister of the congregation with which connection is claimed, or to the minister of the parish within which the parents reside, or to the Clerk of the Presbytery involved so that he may pass these to whoever is responsible and that they may be entered in a Baptismal Register. In a case of adult baptism, of course, it is not likely there would be urgency and the pattern outlined above for confirmation should be followed.

Teachers of Religious Education in Schools

Ministers of the Church of Scotland who have taken up posts as full-time teachers of Religious Education in Schools, or who have been appointed by Education Committees of Regional Councils as full-time Advisers in Religious Education, are entitled to sit in Presbytery, provided they renew the vows of their ordination and sign the Formula. The crave of a petitioner who is a Licentiate and who acts as a Teacher of Religious Education in a School that he might be ordained in that office was rejected by a recent General Assembly.

All of these appointments are, naturally, completely outwith the jurisdiction and control of the Church; the teacher taking his orders exclusively from the Education Committee which employs him through the agency of the head teacher of the school where he is employed. An interesting situation could arise were it to be reported that a minister of the Church of Scotland, employed as just such a teacher, was blatantly instilling heretical doctrine into the minds of children under his care. The Presbytery concerned would presumably begin by an appeal to the minister himself and if this fell on deaf or hostile ears it could make representations to the Education Committee, but if that body was not prepared to take effective action the best the Presbytery could do would be to pursue the minister *qua* ministerial member of Presbytery and, if he persisted in his evil courses, to depose him from the ministry. In other words, the Church cannot stop heretical doctrine being taught in schools, but it can make sure it is not taught by ministers of the Church of Scotland!

The same kind of considerations would in my view apply *mutatis mutandis* to Directors of Religious Broadcasting.

Administrative Posts

There are a limited number of posts of a secretarial and administrative character in the Church to which ministers are appointed, usually by the General Assembly, although some are made at the will of the Committee. Such appointments can be made today only after the position has been 'cleared' with the Assembly Council.

Strange as it may seem, the Principal Clerk of Assembly was, until 1961, a parish minister who undertook this extra commitment. In that year the office was converted into a full-time one, including also the Secretaryship of the General Administration Committee and of the Judicial Commission, the person also to act as Secretary to the Moderator of the General Assembly. There are also today ministers engaged by the Board of Stewardship and Finance (one), the Department of Ministry and Mission (four), the Board of Social Responsibility (two), the Board of World Mission and Unity (five) and the Board of Education (nine, which includes two teaching at St Colm's). There are also two full-time Presbytery Clerks appointed by, paid by and answerable to, their own courts.

All of these have seats in Presbytery.

9

Leaving the Ministry

There are only three ways in which one may cease to be a minister—by death, deposition or voluntary relinquishment accepted by a court of the Church. One's ministry in a parish, on the other hand, may be brought to a close by death or at the will of the minister with consent of Presbytery, by translation or demission, or at the will of the Presbytery alone or of a superior court as a consequence of proceedings taken under the Act anent Congregations in an Unsatisfactory State or under the Act anent Congregations in Changed Circumstances. I shall look at each of them in turn.

Demission of Status–But first a word on the subject of status. There is, strange as it may seem, no legislation that enables a minister to offer, or authorises a Presbytery to accept, the resignation of his status as a minister. There is provision whereby he may be deprived of this, but none allowing him to volunteer to relinquish it. The late Principal Clerk, J B Longmuir, had an ingenious—and probably accurate—explanation in the suggestion that to our forefathers the mere fact that a man had come to form so low an opinion of the ministry that he wished to leave it, provided adequate reason for depriving him of it—and so the result was achieved by judicial process! The position today is that if for personal reasons a minister wishes to cease being a minister—he will need to do this should he decide to contest a Parliamentary seat (*p* 135)—then he offers his resignation to his Presbytery which, after satisfying itself that he is acting responsibly, can be counted upon to accept. His status can be restored only by the General Assembly.

By Death

On the occasion of the death of a minister of a parish, the Presbytery meets within the premises of his Church on the day of his funeral. This is properly a meeting *pro re nata* but it does not need to be officially called by the Moderator or approved by the Presbytery, although today it is customary for notice to be given by newspaper advertisement. At this meeting an Interim Moderator is appointed, and also where appropriate arrangements are made to cover the supply of the pulpit, an interim arrangement may be approved for the carrying on of a chaplaincy or other similar commitment, and generally any other urgent business arising in consequence of the death is attended to. The Interim Moderator will formally declare the charge vacant on the first, or at the latest the first convenient, Sunday thereafter (*p* 148), the vacancy having actually occurred on the day of death.

Since the minister who has just died had not a minister of his own, it is for the Presbytery to take charge of the conduct of the Funeral Service, although this, naturally, is not part of the Presbytery meeting. In keeping the record it is customary to say that the Presbytery 'met in terms of Act XX 1931 consequent on the death of Mr AB', and after the close of the formal minute to add a footnote to the effect that 'The Funeral Service was conducted by.... and the Burial took place at ...'.

In the case of the death of a retired minister or of one employed in capacity other than in the ministry of a parish, the arrangements are in the hands of his own minister in consultation with the next-of-kin, and while members of Presbytery will no doubt wish to attend, they do so not as a court. In either case, at its first ordinary meeting after the death, the Presbytery will record the deletion from its Roll and fitting tribute will be paid.

By Deposition

Deposition is one of the most solemn censures of the Church, surpassed only by excommunication, and it involves banishment from the ministry as well as the severance of the pastoral tie with a particular charge or the termination of a non-parochial appointment. A deposed minister cannot hold the office of an elder. Deposition is a sentence which may be imposed by Presbytery, Synod or General Assembly and follows upon a legal process known as 'libel' in which a minister, probationer or deaconess has been accused of some gross misconduct or of some serious heresy and this has been proved to the satisfaction of the court concerned.

Process of Libel

The term 'libel' is applied in the Church of Scotland to the formal indictment by which a minister, probationer or deaconess is charged with misconduct or heresy. In the present context I am proposing to look at the process as it applies to a minister whether or not he holds a charge. In all normal circumstances the process of libel will be begun by the Presbytery. That is not necessarily so, for the Assembly themselves have in the past been known to initiate such an action, as, for example, when it was alleged that on the previous day an intoxicated commissioner had attempted to enter the Hall and had been in the same condition in the streets, the Assembly instituted the action but passed the papers to his Presbytery to proceed in the matter. Or one can imagine the Assembly taking action were a minister in course of a debate to make a speech which was deemed to be seriously heretical. Such possibilities are today, I am sure, largely of academic interest and we may safely assume that the Presbytery will be the court of first instance.

The whole proceedings are now governed by a very comprehensive Act of 1935.

Fama—Action will be taken by a Presbytery following a *fama*, that is, a scandalous report concerning a minister within its bounds. It is not necessary that he be a member of Presbytery, it is enough that he enjoys ministerial status and resides within the bounds. If he lives elsewhere the matter has to be officially reported to the Presbytery under whose supervision he is, giving a full account of the situation as known, a list of witnesses, and any papers or other productions. Presbyteries are warned against proceeding hastily or rashly in a concern of such importance and such delicacy. It is not enough that someone should make an accusation, that person must either lay a charge in writing, or in presence of the Presbytery he must make an oral accusation, giving an account of its probability and undertaking to produce evidence in its support. I should myself imagine that the latter requirement would be met were the accuser to appear before a Committee of Presbytery duly authorised to deal with the matter rather than before the whole court. It may be, of course, that the scandal has reached a very wide public, has become a *fama clamosa*, and in that case the Presbytery may for its own vindication find it necessary to proceed even in the absence of an accuser. If the events that form the substance of the *fama* are more than five years old, it will be only in very exceptional circumstances that the Presbytery will take action.

Preliminary Enquiry—The first duty of the Presbytery is to give to the person concerned notice of what is afoot and then to conduct, through a Committee, a Preliminary Enquiry. The accused person is entitled to be present throughout this enquiry and to be given full opportunity to defend himself. If in the light of the findings of this enquiry the Presbytery resolves it should proceed no further, then the accuser (who should be at the bar) has a right of appeal to the Synod, or if the Presbytery had proceeded *ex proprio motu* then any member of Presbytery is at liberty to take the matter to the Synod by dissent and complaint.

Statement—If as a result of the Preliminary Enquiry the Presbytery resolves to proceed to trial, a Statement is to be prepared setting forth in precise terms the heretical opinions or the improper conduct alleged, and this is to be served on the accused with a request that he indicate in writing whether he admits or denies each of the various allegations. It is in order at this point for the accused to state in writing Objections to the terms, or to the sufficiency, of the Statement, and the Presbytery after due consultation may amend or add to the Statement, or may resolve to adhere to it as framed.

Plea of Guilty—'If the person concerned shall admit any or all of the allegations contained in said Statement the Presbytery shall take such steps as may seem to it to be necessary and proper according to the nature and extent of the allegations admitted by such person.' If in his answers to the Statement the accused tenders a plea of Guilty on all of the counts, then the Presbytery should meet at once to dispose of the matter. It will hear a report of what has happened, will resolve to accept the plea, and before going on to consider sentence will hear a plea in mitigation submitted either by the accused or by another on his behalf. For the further action which the Presbytery may take at this point, see page 225.

Preparation of Libel—If the allegations or any of them are denied the Presbytery proceeds towards trial by libel. The libel is prepared in name of the Presbytery, but before it is served on the accused it should be submitted to the Procurator of the Church for revision. In its final form it is subscribed by the Moderator and Clerk of the Presbytery.

The Court—The Presbytery has some options in

the matter of how the case is to be conducted. It may resolve to sit as a court and hear the case, or it may remit the matter with powers to a Committee of not less than three and not more than five, or it may remit to a Committee as above but with the addition of two persons from the Board of Assessors appointed in terms of the Act by the Board of Practice and Procedure. Whichever course is followed, the resultant body will form 'the court' for purposes of the trial. The Presbytery is to appoint either two or three of its number with the duty of acting as prosecutors, and both they and the accused are at liberty to engage professional counsel.

Special Defence—Within 21 days of the service of the libel the accused may enter a Special Defence (alibi, for example, or insanity, or diminished responsibility), and since in respect of this the *onus probandi* will fall upon him, he should submit a list of witnesses whom he proposes to call in support. He has the right to borrow any documents that are to be produced against him.

Relevance—At the first sitting of the court the accused is invited to state Objections to the competency or relevance of the charge. Should the charge be one of heresy this will be the crucial point in the trial, for the defence may be expected to be that the words or sentiments complained of were not in fact heretical. In a misconduct case it is the facts that are likely to be challenged, whereas in a heresy case the fact of what exactly was said is likely to be admitted (the accused may very happily supply the court with a transcript of the sermon or other speech in which it is alleged heretical

opinions appear). In a heresy case, then, it is likely
to be around this preliminary plea that the whole
argument will centre. If the court finds the
relevance of the charge or charges to be established it will normally be in a position to pronounce
verdict at this point, whereas in a misconduct case
it is only the beginning, for the court will have to
go on and hear evidence on the facts. If on the
other hand the court finds that the relevance of the
libel has not been sustained, then the accused will
be exonerated and the whole business departed
from.

Diet of Proof—If the libel, having been found
relevant, is still denied by the accused, the court is
to fix a time and place for holding a diet of proof.
At this diet all evidence is to be given on oath, first
that for the prosecution, then that for the defence,
each side having the right to cross-examine and to
re-examine, and the whole evidence is to be taken
down in shorthand and extended, the shorthand
writer having taken the oath *de fideli*. Both sides are
then to be given an opportunity of addressing the
court.

Report to Presbytery—When the court consists of a
Committee it has to report its findings on the
entire matter, including its findings on the facts, to
the whole Presbytery, but if it so desires it may take
some time to consider matters before thus reporting. If its findings in fact are unanimous, they are
final (as far as the Presbytery is concerned) and
cannot be reversed or altered by that court. Where
unanimity has not been achieved, the state of the
vote is to be reported and the Presbytery is to
decide whether to accept the majority view or to

have the evidence printed and itself to hear the parties anew before reaching its own judgment.

Censure—If on the whole issue the verdict of the whole Presbytery is that the libel has been proven wholly or in part, or if, as has been explained above, a plea of Guilty has been tendered, the Presbytery is to proceed to consider sentence. Before doing so it is to afford opportunity to the accused or his representative to submit a plea in mitigation of the offence.

The censures of the Church are admonition, rebuke, suspension from office, deposition and excommunication. In a case which had been sufficiently serious to merit proceeding by libel, it is unlikely that admonition would be considered a sufficient sentence, although it might well be that rebuke was felt adequate, depending on the nature of the offence and the whole circumstances surrounding it. In a case of heretical teaching, for example, it might be thought good to reprove the offender for his conduct and enjoin him to be careful that it be not repeated.

Suspension and deposition differ mainly in their duration, the former being for a period (although it may be *sine die*) while the latter is once and for all. They differ also in that the court which imposes the suspension can lift it, whereas if a minister is deposed then although it was the Presbytery which deposed him it is only the General Assembly which can restore him. Where there is hope that in time the offender will be restored, there is much to be said in favour of suspension *sine die*, for in this case status may be restored without the necessity for the whole miserable facts to be rehearsed in a petition for restoration presented to the Assembly—which is the only way back for the person deposed.

'Excommunication or exclusion from the fellowship of the Church is resorted to only in cases of peculiar aggravation, when all other means of reclaiming the offender have failed, and when he continues impenitent and contumacious.' It must be a long time indeed since such a sentence was last pronounced in the Kirk.

Temporary Suspension—At the point when the libel has been found relevant, or at any time thereafter, the Presbytery may enjoin the accused to abstain from the exercise of all ministerial functions until the case has been disposed of. During such time the Presbytery has to arrange for the work of the parish to proceed and will do so by appointing an Interim Moderator and so on as in a case of leave of absence. The minister's right to stipend, manse and all other benefits of the living, will be in no way affected by such temporary suspension. The Act does not in terms provide for this—indeed it could be argued that it by implication prohibits it—but I imagine the Presbytery would be justified in taking this step at an even earlier stage in the case of a *fama clamosa* where the scandal was so acute that to allow the man to continue his ministry would itself be a scandal. It would be most unfortunate were a minister under shadow of trial for some heinous offence to be carrying on his normal parish duties.

Proceedings in Civil Courts—It is well established that the courts of the Church cannot found upon verdicts pronounced in criminal courts or upon judgments given in civil courts but must reach their own judgments upon the evidence which is brought before them. A very real difficulty can arise in these circumstances. Let it be, for example, that a minister is accused of embezzlement from some trust fund that was under his control, and let it be that a considerable sum is involved. Obviously the courts both of the land and of the Church have an interest and are under obligation to prosecute. But it is the police and not the Presbytery who have the power to impound all the documentary evidence and to keep this very firmly under their own—or the Procurator Fiscal's—control until after the criminal trial. This is likely to be a very long time indeed. In the absence of this vital evidence the Presbytery has no hope of establishing a libel. If the accused is found Guilty in the Sheriff Court and sentenced to a fair period of imprisonment then no action can profitably be taken by the Presbytery until he is once more at liberty and free to attend meetings. If he still staunchly maintains his innocence—he was 'framed' by the police—what is the Presbytery to do? It is to be presumed that at the time of his arrest, the Presbytery put him under temporary suspension in terms of the paragraph above, but the congregation will have an understandable reluctance to continue paying stipend to a minister while he is awaiting trial, and even more so while he is serving a term of imprisonment. It is a real predicament.

I have to confess that I do not know the answer. But let it not be thought that the question is a purely hypothetical one since I met with just such a case in actual fact. Fortunately from the Church's point of view the minister concerned, although loudly proclaiming his innocence, was persuaded when the scandal first broke to resign his charge on grounds of ill-health. But he need not have done so. At the end of the day—that is, more than two years later—the Presbytery having got the documents from the police and the offender being once more at liberty, a libel was prepared, a plea of Guilty was tendered, and the minister was suspended *sine die*. As I say, it need not have worked out so comparatively simply.

Record Apart—With a view to keeping the ordinary records of the courts free from the presence of undesirable matter and to prevent later mutilation through deletions, it is provided that in all cases where moral delinquency is alleged the Presbytery is to resolve to keep the proceedings in the case in a Record Apart. When the final judgment has involved censure in any degree the Presbytery is to enter in its regular Minute-book the first minute of the Record Apart, the libel (or at least a summary of its charges), and the final judgment. When the case has ended in acquittal, the Record Apart, along with all the papers in the case, is to be sealed up in a package which will be held *in retentis* for five years and then destroyed.

Appeal

There may be three parties to an action of this kind any one of whom has a right to take the matter further by appeal. First, the accused person obviously has such a right. Second, the original complainer, that is, the person who laid the *fama* in the first place, also has a right of appeal. And third, any member of Presbytery dissatisfied with how things have gone has the right to dissent and complain. Such appeal must be to the Synod although it may be taken on from there to the Assembly, and if the latter court is due to meet earlier than the former it goes there direct.

Appeal may be taken at any point in the course of the proceedings—the accused may appeal against the decision of the court to hear a certain witness, or he may appeal against the court's finding on relevance—but the Presbytery will press on in face of all such appeals right up to and including the pronouncing of sentence. When this stage has been reached, appeal must again be taken and this will have the effect of sisting proceedings so that the Presbytery will not go on to implement the sentence unless and until the case has been finally disposed of in its favour. If it stops short of sentence then when its verdict is upheld it has to take the matter up afresh so that sentence may be passed.

The Judicial Commission–Appeal, although it may be taken to the General Assembly will not be heard by that court—unless it be an appeal against sentence alone. The General Assembly, as a court, is well qualified to deal with large questions of principle regarding the behaviour of its ministers; it is ill-equipped to reach judgment on the question of how far the behaviour of any particular minister has measured up to these standards. I need not enlarge on the disadvantages from which it suffers in this regard. Suffice to say that at a time when libel cases were regularly on the Assembly agenda, it was no uncommon thing for a very weary court to be reaching a judgment affecting the whole future of a minister at an advanced hour of the morning long after they should all have been tucked up in bed and when the judgment of the most clear-headed was not a little impaired from long incarceration in conditions not of the most comfortable. The whole business, it was felt, left a great deal to be desired.

So in 1940 an Act was passed setting up a completely new piece of machinery. The business of hearing libel cases (other than heresy) was to be taken right out of the hands of the General Assembly and put into those of a body called the Judicial Commission, consisting of 48 ministers and elders with a quorum of 24 but subject to the restriction that 'no appeal is to be begun unless at least 30 members are present at the commencement thereof'. In 1985 the Assembly declared the whole proceedings of the Commission inept in a case where, by inadvertance, it had begun a hearing with only 29 present, and that in spite of the fact that more than a quorum had been present throughout the entire proceedings. The appellant has at the outset of the proceedings the right to object to any member of the Commission sitting in his case, but he must so object 'at the commencement of the hearing of the appeal' and must show cause for his complaint. The other members present are sole judges as to whether the complaint should be sustained, their decision not being subject to review. An interesting question arises as to whether for the purpose of the '30-present' rule the appeal is to be deemed to have 'begun' before or after such complaint has been taken.

The Commission has the duty to hear and

determine appeals coming up from the lower courts in cases by libel affecting the character and conduct of ministers (but not in a heresy case) but it has no power to propose, determine or pronounce sentences or penalties, only to come to a conclusion on facts. The Commission enjoys all the powers of the Assembly in the matter of compelling the attendance of witnesses, of taking evidence on oath and of calling for the production of documents. The hearing goes on day after day until it is concluded, although power is given to adjourn the hearing should the justice of the case so demand.

Minutes—'The Minutes of the Judicial Commission shall enumerate each count in the libel ... and shall show the Finding of the Commission on each count and the grounds on which the Finding has been reached. The Minutes shall also show the state of the vote of the Members of the Commission on each count.' When the hearing is concluded the minutes are to be engrossed in a Sederunt Book, signed by the Chairman, and reported to the next General Assembly. When the minutes are before the Assembly an opportunity will be given for questions. The Moderator is then to ask in regard to each Finding, 'Do the General Assembly approve this Finding of the Judicial Commission "Yes" or "No"?' and the Assembly are to vote without debate.

Sentence—If the Findings be against the accused he may be heard by himself or his agent in mitigation and the Assembly will then proceed to consider whether the sentence imposed by the lower court is appropriate and should be sustained, or whether some other sentence should be substituted.

Comment—I have personally no recollection of any libel case having been dealt with under this legislation. In 1960 the powers of the Judicial Committee were extended to include procedure under the Act anent Congregations in an Unsatisfactory State and a few of these cases have of recent years reached the Assembly, but none concerned with a case of libel. Two general comments might be offered.

First, that it is difficult to envisage the Findings of the Judicial Commission being successfully challenged in the Assembly. Presumably if the Findings ran counter to the facts to an outrageous degree, the Assembly might dissociate themselves from them; but since the Assembly's knowledge of the facts is wholly that which is supplied to them by the Commission, it seems most unlikely that such a situation could arise. It seems a pity, therefore, that this little drama should have to be played out, for if there is one thing the Assembly resent more than another it is the suspicion that they are being used as a rubber-stamp—they will show the most amazing ingenuity in investing themselves with powers. The 'Unsatisfactory State' cases that have recently come up have amply illustrated this. It would seem simpler—and much more realistic— were the Committee vested with complete and final authority in the matter of the Findings. If this is not acceptable then some machinery must be devised whereby the Assembly can themselves deal with the business in a meaningful way. At the moment we fall between two stools.

Second, it is very difficult for a court which has not heard the case in all its detail to judge how adequate or appropriate the sentence may be. It is true that under our jury trial system one body reaches a verdict and sentence is determined by another. But while he had no part in reaching the verdict, the judge had heard every word of the evidence. That is not so under the Judicial Commission procedure and to me that seems unfortunate. Again as the 'Unsatisfactory State' cases showed questions will be asked designed to start a retrial. And when this is ruled out of order a bad taste will be left.

By Translation

Translation is the technical term applied to the situation where a minister is moved from one pastoral charge to another whether or not within the same Presbytery. It is not applicable where a minister moves to a pastoral charge from some form of extra-parochial appointment—in such a case he simply relinquishes his post and is inducted to the parish as a Minister Without Charge; nor does it apply when a minister moves from a parish to take up some other post within the jurisdiction of the Church—in such a case he seeks permission to demit his charge in order to take up the other appointment. At one time the word was applied to the movement of a minister from a charge in the Presbyterian Church of England to a Church of Scotland charge, but that was clearly a misuse of the term.

When the minister elected to a vacant charge

J

within its bounds is minister of a parish elsewhere, it will fall to the Presbytery to sustain the election, and having done this it will go on to make provisional arrangements for induction, at the same time instructing the Clerk to forward the papers (including the Call) to the Clerk of the Presbytery of which the person elected is a member. It used to be almost universal practice that the Presbytery appointed commissioners to 'prosecute the call' before the other Presbytery; and indeed when this was not done, a very humble apology was sent expressing the hope that the failure to send commissioners would not be construed as a discourtesy. Today, I imagine, courtesy is manifested in not sending commissioners!

The practice clearly was a survival from the day when a translation might be contested, and its object was to ensure that the interest of the calling Presbytery would be represented by there being someone present to defend the case in favour of translation. The minister's congregation is cited and can, if so determined, argue a case in defence of his staying put. The chances of this today are not very great, and in any case the 1984 Act provides that in the event of the Presbytery resolving not to translate, the calling Presbytery, although it was not represented at the bar, has ten days in which to take appeal and to lodge reasons therefor.

At the *in hunc effectum* meeting of Presbytery for the induction of a minister being translated it is for the Clerk to lay on the table an extract Minute of the releasing Presbytery wherein that court has agreed to translate Mr AB to the Parish of X,

has instructed him to await the orders of the
Presbytery of Q as to his induction thereto, and has
declared that until said induction he remains
minister of the Parish of Y. Intimation of the
induction is immediately sent to the Clerk of the
releasing Presbytery and the name is removed
from its Roll.

By Demission

A Minister who has been inducted to a parish
cannot by any unilateral action of his own, or even
by any mutual agreement with the congregation or
its office-bearers, bring to an end the relationship
created by induction. Only the Presbytery which
forged the link has power to dissolve it. This it does
by agreeing to a request from the minister for
permission to demit his charge, fixing a date for
this, and appointing an Interim Moderator to act
in the anticipated vacancy. Whether the desire to
go is based on reasons of age or health or is with a
view to taking up some other appointment, or to
moving to some other denomination, or to leaving
altogether the service of the Church, the only way
out is by demission. There is an increasing tendency to refer to the man who goes on grounds of
age or health as 'retiring' and this in everyday
language is an accurate enough description of
what he is doing. Technically, however, he is
demitting. As to the position of the minister who
takes the law into his own hands and departs, he is
to be treated as in desertion and is to be deposed
(*p* 98).

For Reason of Age or Infirmity

For very many years the needs of all ministers who demitted because of age or on grounds of ill health were looked after by the 'Aged and Infirm Ministers' Fund' and the term 'aged and infirm' has come to stay. When I use the expression here it is meant to refer to the case of the minister giving up because he feels the restraint of age or that his health has reached the stage when he should bring his active ministry to a close.

Timing—A minister who sees himself approaching this stage should take early opportunity of having a talk with the Presbytery Clerk with a view, among other things, to working out a time-table of events. It is important that before he finally commits himself to demission he should be perfectly clear as to where he stands in the matter of pension rights, and in fact he should have in his hand a Minute from the Retirement Scheme Committee covering the question of such entitlement. It is a sound rule never to take anything for granted in this field. So as to set the ball rolling, his application for a pension should be submitted to the Presbytery for approval and for transmission to the Assembly Committee. Since this involves securing the concurrence of his Kirk Session it is important that he should at this point be prepared for the fact that his going will become common knowledge. It is possible also that he may be hopeful of securing a loan from the Housing and Loan Fund to assist him in purchasing a house for his retirement, and an application in this connection should also be lodged as soon as the decision to go has been reached.

It can be most helpful also to have an early opportunity of looking at the overall readjustment situation in the area and considering how this may be affected by the forthcoming vacancy. Until the passing of the 1984 Readjustment Act it used to be that a minister could be seen as retiring in the interest of readjustment only if the approach had come to him from the side of the Presbytery, for immediately after he took the initiative by intimating his intention of demitting he disqualified himself from any of the benefits that might follow from readjustment. This could be grossly unfair in that if two neighbouring ministers were both approaching retiring age and a union in fact followed the retirement of one of them, the minister who had initiated the move got nothing, the other might often get a very great deal. The new Act has altered that, and in such a case nowadays both may benefit. It is therefore very worthwhile having a look at the whole position before taking any irrevocable action.

Since legislation now allows vacancy procedure to be initiated while the minister is still in his charge, there is much to be said for seeking permission to demit quite a few months before the date envisaged for departure. Fixing these two dates—for the Presbytery to deal with the demission and for the minister to go—is also a matter to be discussed with the Presbytery Clerk. The gap between the two dates should not be too great, for it can be very trying to go around the parish taking farewell of folk for months on end, but a reasonable interval can help greatly in getting the formalities of the vacancy out of the way before the congregation is left pastorless.

Release—At whatever time is finally agreed, the minister submits through the Presbytery Clerk a letter in which he asks leave to demit on the grounds of age or infirmity as the case may be, and if the latter is the reason, medical evidence should be included in support of the application. This letter will be laid on the table at the first meeting of Presbytery after receipt when it will be agreed that the matter be dealt with at the following meeting, and the Clerk will be instructed to cite the congregation for its interest. At that next meeting the minister will be asked if he adheres to his request and the congregational representatives will be asked if they concur, after which the Presbytery will agree to accept the demission as from whatever date has been agreed. It will also be resolved that the minister retain his seat in Presbytery, or, if he is to be moving out of the district, that he be given a Presbyterial Certificate.

Presbytery Connection—It used to be that whether he wanted it or not a minister who retired in this way had a seat in Presbytery, and that if moved to another district he could transfer that seat only on petition to the Synod of the welcoming Presbytery. Two Acts of 1980 altered the position here, the one by allowing a retired minister to resign his seat on application to the Presbytery, and the other by providing for transference to another Presbytery merely on application to that Presbytery whose decision on the matter is final. The minister has to lodge a Presbyterial Certificate and a Certificate of Status.

Congregational Attachment—Should a minister on demitting his charge continue his membership of his former congregation? There is no law on the subject, but my answer is an emphatic 'No'. In fairness to his successor, to his former members, and in the long run to himself, a minister, when his ministry in a charge comes to an end, should (with his wife) dissociate himself completely from the life of that congregation; and he is well advised to do so during the vacancy, and most certainly before the induction of the new minister. I am convinced beyond any shadow of a doubt that only harm to the cause and hurt to innocent people can result from his staying on—even if 'only till the new man is settled in'.

It is inevitable that members of a congregation will turn to the minister under whom they have grown up rather than to the young fellow who has recently arrived and whom they have not yet met— 'It would be so nice for Mr X to take Jean's wedding, you see he baptised her. I am sure the new minister will understand'. And from the other side, if you have been minister of a parish for 30 years and are still living in the neighbourhood it is difficult, when you hear of the death of one who had been very close to you, not to drop in to express sympathy—but you may do so before your successor has so much as heard of the death. The awkward situations that can arise are numberless, and the one sure way to evade them is to be at a safe distance. It may be asking a lot—you may think it is asking too much—to expect a minister, on demitting, to move out of the district where he has spent so large a part of his life and where so many of his interests lie. It is certainly not asking too much that he and his wife should get out of the congregation and should stay well away from it. The best way to achieve that is to become actively integrated into the life of some other congregation. The law provides that a retired minister may be associated in the practical work of the Kirk Session of the congregation of which he is a member: common sense dictates it should not be that of his former charge.

All of the above seems so obviously right and reasonable. What I have never been able to understand—and I have come across it so often over the years—is how otherwise highly intelligent and responsible people fail to see it when applied to their own case. I think it would be no bad thing were it made a condition of Presbytery's accepting a demission that, along with his Presbyterial Certificate, the minister was to be given his 'lines' to enable him and his wife to join some other congregation—and to do so at that very stage.

In Connection with Readjustment

When it is a condition of some Basis of Readjustment that a minister is to demit his charge in order to allow some union or linking to take place and the minister in question has in writing agreed to the terms of the said Basis, there is no need for him to make formal application for permission to demit or for the Presbytery to take any further action in the in matter. Such a minister is to be regarded as retiring in the interest of readjustment and he consequently retains his seat in Presbytery. As a courtesy, of course, the Presbytery will want to take note of his going and to wish him well in his retirement.

A curious situation can arise in this context. In almost every case, demission in the interest of readjustment simply means 'early retirement'. This need not be so, however, and cases have occurred where a minister in his early years, having retired to facilitate a union, has taken up employment outwith the Church. He is still entitled to retain a seat in Presbytery.

To Take Up Another Appointment

As indicated earlier, a minister who has received a call to a congregation in another denomination, or who has been appointed to some post within the service of the Church, must, before moving to such a charge or appointment, receive permission of Presbytery to demit his present charge. As in the above case he will submit a letter asking leave to demit as from a certain date in order to....and this will be laid on the table and agreement reached that it will be dealt with at next meeting and the congregation cited thereto, proceedings thereafter being precisely as above. It will depend upon the nature of the appointment whether or not the minister is entitled to a seat in Presbytery. If he is going to another denomination or to another Presbytery, it should also be agreed that he be given a Presbyterial Certificate testifying that he leaves with the status of a minister of the Church of Scotland and that his character and conduct are in every respect becoming to his profession. The date fixed for demission will normally be the date of his taking up his new post.

To Leave the Service of the Church

When a minister of a parish intimates a desire to leave the service of the Church, for whatever ostensible reason, his letter is to be laid on the table and, simultaneously with agreeing that the matter be dealt with at the next meeting, the Presbytery is to appoint one or more of its number to meet with the minister concerned and to confer with him regarding his reasons for taking this step. This is an important provision that should be scrupulously adhered to. In most cases the reasons will be found to be perfectly 'reasonable', but the occasion does arise when a young man has been subjected to pressures from within the congregation, or when he has got to the stage of feeling helpless and alone and has lost heart, or when he is beginning to doubt his sense of vocation. It is very sad that anyone should have been allowed to reach this stage; it would be nothing short of tragic were he to be lost to the service of the Church for want of somebody to stand by him with a word of advice and encouragement. There is the possibility too that the minister wishing to go has reached that point where he should seriously consider whether he can conscientiously continue within the ministry or should rather be thinking of demitting status. This is a matter that could profitably be discussed with the Presbytery Committee. In either of these types of cases the Presbytery has a very real pastoral responsibility. When the matter of the demission is taken up at the next meeting, the first item will be to receive a report from this committee.

When it is agreed that a minister should demit in a case where he is leaving the service of the

Church, it should also be decided whether or not he is to be given a certificate that will entitle him to continue to perform the functions of the ministry. He will not be entitled to a seat in Presbytery except in the special case discussed above (*p* 241).

Avoidance of Libel—It not infrequently happens that a minister who has been involved in some discreditable conduct takes the initiative, and, before the Presbytery can begin any action in connection with a *fama*, tenders the resignation of his charge on grounds of health. He will usually have no difficulty supplying a medical certificate testifying that he is under strain and would benefit from being relieved from the responsibilities of his office. It is likely he will also indicate that he has no intention of asking for a Presbyterial Certificate. What is the Presbytery to do in such a case? It is very tempting to take things at face value, to accept the demission and avoid a process which is sure to be both difficult and unpleasant. The congregation will be more than happy to let it go at that—they are being saved from what could prove a messy situation. Nor will there be lacking those who will see it as the path of Christian charity to allow the issue to be evaded in this way. As the law stands at present (changes are envisaged) the Presbytery may withhold a Presbyterial Certificate when asked for one 'if it sees cause to withhold the same'— this without any formal accusation having been framed. So far as the record is concerned, there-fore, the situation will be that the minister has demitted his charge on grounds of ill health and that a Presbyterial Certificate has been withheld (without reason stated).

The present Act governing Certificates goes on to say that 'in the event of a Presbyterial Certificate being withheld, the minister concerned may, after the expiry of at least two years from the date when it was withheld, make application for the same to the Presbytery which formerly withheld it, and that Presbytery may ... issue a Presbyterial Certificate in his favour'. Let it be that our hypothetical minister, after four years, applies for a Certificate with a view to finding himself a new charge. It may well have been that the scandal at the time of demission was of a nature that would almost certainly have led to deposition, and from recollection of this the Presbytery may well be hesitant, or indeed completely unwilling, to issue a Certificate. The minister concerned is now, however, in a position of strength from which he can claim that either he should be given a Certificate or that there should be proved against him misconduct sufficient to justify its being withheld, and to do so secure in the knowledge that no-one is wanting to revive an old scandal, and that even if they were, the chance of their being able to make a libel stick after so long a passage of time would be remote in the extreme.

To me it has always seemed that in a case of this kind the Presbytery should be hesitant to let the *fama* go completely by default, that at the very least it should accept demission only after some kind of admission had been made which could go on the record. And the Presbytery should formally resolve that it was withholding a Certificate even if none had been asked for. It has always been a contention of mine that there is no shame in having dirty linen—the shame lies in never being seen taking it to the laundry.

By Severance

Unsatisfactory State

During the 1950s there developed in one of our parishes a situation which was giving cause for grave concern. A minister and his congregation had, from a few days after his induction, got completely at loggerheads, so badly so that not only was the work in that particular congregation being frustrated, but the whole witness of the Kirk within a wide area round about was suffering. The minister was a very able man and one to whom no faintest breath of scandal could conceivably attach; in happier circumstances he could have proved an admirable minister. But things had gone sour at the level of his personal relations within the congregation. It had all started simply enough and then one silly thing had led to another until the cumulative effect had become quite disastrous and all efforts at achieving a solution by friendly approaches to both sides had miserably failed. He appeared latterly to spend most of his time working out clever ways of outstripping the Presbytery in their efforts to grapple with the situation. Things had reached the stage of being a public scandal and it was clear to everyone— except, apparently to the minister—that there could be no improvement as long as he continued there. He had no inclination to move to another parish—he would have seen it as a dereliction of duty—and in any case he had by this time acquired a reputation that would have guaranteed his not being considered in any vacancy. Something had to be done.

Act of 1960–The result was the appearance on the Statute Book in 1960 of an Act anent Congregations in an Unsatisfactory State. It is made perfectly clear that it does not apply when the appropriate action would be trial by libel or in the case of the insanity of a minister. It was aimed not at impropriety but at incompatibility. It was, of course, designed to deal with the general situation where a serious breakdown of relations had occurred between minister and people rather than merely to cope with one particular case. The ink was scarcely dry, however, before it was put into operation in the particular case above, and yet it took three years, with endless reporting and resolving in the Presbytery, with two full days spent by the Judicial Commission, and after a long debate in the General Assembly, before it was possible to dissolve the pastoral tie and have the congregation declared vacant. Having thus achieved its immediate objective, the Act seemed to have been laid aside, for one did not hear of its having been invoked, and certainly no case reached the Assembly until a few years ago when quite a trickle of cases emerged. These were all cases which had been appealed to the Judicial Commission and I think it would be true to say that in each case Assembly commissioners were left with a feeling of some unhappiness. Justice had probably been done, but it was not very obvious that it was so. In 1985 it was remitted to the Board of Practice and Procedure to look afresh at the legislation, and this it has been doing.

Procedure—When it comes to the knowledge of a Presbytery as a result of quinquennial visitation, on a petition from within the congregation, or on other good grounds that all is not well in the life of one of its congregations, it is the duty of the Presbytery by visitation to acquaint itself with the facts, and by counsel and consultation to try to set things right. If this fails—and if things have got thus far the chances of success must be slender— the committee reports to the Presbytery that in its view the congregation is in an unsatisfactory state and that this is substantially due to faults personal to the minister (or it may be to some member or office-bearer, but for present purposes it is with the case of the minister alone that we are concerned). If the Presbytery agrees with the conclusions of the report it is to organise what amounts to a trial, with power, if the judgments are upheld, to dissolve the pastoral tie and declare the charge vacant. Part of the difficulty emerges right here, for we talk and think of a 'trial', and yet it is not fault far less crime that is being investigated but just incompatibility, inadequacy, insensitivity. Procedure continues on the model of the trial, the minister having a right of appeal to the Judicial Commission which proceeds much as in a case of libel (*p* 229) and it is then for the Assembly to receive the report of the Commission, to hear a plea in mitigation, and thereafter to uphold the judgment of the Presbytery, or to do otherwise as it deems fit. In 1985 an appeal from the north was upheld on the grounds of irregularity in the procedure of the Presbytery. One cannot but wonder what the condition of relationships within the congregation would be after all that had happened. If minister and people had not been able to 'make a go' of things starting with all the goodwill and enthusiasm that go with an induction, what hope was there in a situation like this?

A *New Act*–The Board of Practice and Procedure presented proposals to the 1986 Assembly, and these in the form of an Overture are at the time of writing with the Presbyteries for consideration. A new Act, it is hoped, will go down under the Barrier Act in 1987 and hopefully become law the following year. The proposed new Act adopts a completely fresh starting-point—instead of searching to discover where it may attribute 'fault', it accepts the fact that, for whatever reason, there has been a breakdown in personal relations, and one which is not going to be healed; that accordingly the link between minister and congregation has got to be broken; and that, since the congregation cannot remove, it must be for the minister to do so. It therefore ordains that when in the judgment of a Presbytery after due enquiry a congregation is in an unsatisfactory state (and this is likely to continue unless the minister's tenure is broken), it shall be competent for the Presbytery to terminate such tenure and to declare the charge vacant.

Even if, as one hopes, the Act proves acceptable to Presbyteries, the details of procedure are likely to be amended and adjusted so that it would seem profitless to go into these details at this stage.

Provision for Minister

The 1960 Act says rather airily, 'In all cases in which the pastoral tie is dissolved, the Presbytery shall report to the Maintenance of the Ministry Committee all the circumstances known to it which ought to be in view of the Church in dealing with the question of a maintenance allowance for the minister during such period as he is in receipt of no other regular remuneration, and the Maintenance of the Ministry Committee shall report to the General Assembly, and may make interim payments'. The proposed new Act says simply that the Maintenance of the Ministry Committee 'shall have power to make suitable arrangements for a maintenance allowance, and shall report to the General Assembly thereanent'. This leaves unanswered the vital question, 'Suitable to whom?'

In the case of the minister whose tenure was terminated in 1963 it is believed that he was paid the minimum stipend and given rent-free occupancy of a house until he qualified for a pension. In 1986, on the other hand, the Assembly overwhelmingly refused to consider even a very modest grant-in-aid to a minister whose tenure had been terminated two years previously because he had been in receipt of the minimum stipend for all of that period, during which, of course, he had put himself at the disposal of the Church. It is submitted that any new legislation would do well to be more specific in regard to the provision that is to be made for ministers in such circumstances.

Nor is it a simple problem. These men are ministers, recognised by the Church as qualified for the work of a charge, and in most cases they themselves are highly confident of their ability to discharge the duties of a parish minister—a confidence unhappily not shared by Vacancy Committees who incline to look very narrowly at any minister not in a charge. Such ministers are usually most unwilling to seek employment elsewhere, which in any case is not easy to find in the absence of specialised skills. Ministers who are obliged to seek retirement early because of some physical disability have to survive on a pension. Are men who have been rendered income-less in this way entitled to expect more generous treatment?

Pastoral Care—A novel provision of the draft Act is that any 'termination' is to be immediately reported to the Synod who 'shall arrange for a minister from another Presbytery to give pastoral advice and counsel to the minister, whether or not appeal or dissent and complaint has been taken'. I would not wish to sound cynical, but in my experience an invariable characteristic of ministers who get into this kind of difficulty is that they are not particularly amenable to advice and counsel from any source. Had they been so things might have been different.

By Severance

Changed Circumstances

The rapidly and drastically changing patterns of our modern world have created problems for a Church which was geared to serve a more stable society. There are today in our cities areas which a few years ago had been heavily populated and which are now a sea of red blaes with, perhaps, a disreputable-looking church building standing forlorn and disconsolate in the midst of the desolation. New road-patterns can isolate whole areas with the effect of rendering a church building nearly inaccessible to houses from which it had been used to draw its members. The Act of 1984 anent Congregations in Changed Circumstances was designed to deal with the situation where, because of changed circumstances—such as large-scale movement of population, the emergence of new road patterns, the effects of urban planning, the loss of personnel to provide leadership in the congregation, the age or health of the minister, or other factors outwith the control of the Church— the ends of the ministry are no longer being properly or adequately fulfilled in a particular charge and the situation is unlikely to change for the better. This could have been achieved by putting it into the power of the Presbytery, if so advised, to terminate the minister's tenure and so allow for some form of readjustment being effected.

Procedure—When it becomes clear to a Presbytery that one of its charges has been affected in one of the ways outlined above, it is to appoint a committee to carry out an Enquiry, and that committee is to confer with the Presbytery committee which initiated the matter, with the minister and office-bearers of the congregation concerned, and with such other bodies within and outwith the Church as it considers able to provide relevant information. If satisfied that such a situation exists, the committee is to report accordingly to the Presbytery, copies of the report having been given in advance to all members of Presbytery and to all interested parties. The committee is also to make a recommendation (a) that no action be taken, (b) that changes be made with a view to assisting the congregation, changes of such a kind as can be effected under existing legislation, or (c) 'that since the changed circumstances affecting the congregation and its future are such that the continuance of the congregation as a separate charge can no longer be justified, the minister's tenure should be terminated to allow of an appropriate form of readjustment being immediately effected'.

In fixing a date when the termination is to become effective, the Presbytery is to allow a sufficient period (of up to but not exceeding a year) during which the minister concerned may be expected to have secured a call.

Provision for Minister
When a minister's tenure of his charge has been terminated in this way, he is to receive from the Minimum Stipend Fund a maintenance allowance at the amount of the prevailing minimum stipend as well as the use and occupancy on normal terms of a manse or payment of the full Manse Allowance. Where local funds have become available through the readjustment that has followed on the termination of the tenure, it is for the Presbytery to ensure that the payment to the minister of a maintenance allowance is, as far as possible, made a first charge on such funds. Such provision is, of course, to cease on the minister being inducted to another charge or on obtaining full-time employment outwith the service of the Church; and so

long as the provision continues to be made, the minister is to put himself at the service of the Church in every reasonable way. It may be, of course, that the minister's age will be such that he may be offered acceptable terms for early retirement as in a readjustment case.

In the event of the minister still being without regular income at the end of the two-year period, the whole situation is to be reviewed by the Presbytery in consultation with the minister and the Maintenance of the Ministry Committee.

In Case of Insanity

The case of insanity of a minister constitutes a special case, for while what in effect has to occur is tantamount to demission the circumstances are such as to put it out of the power of the minister to concur in the proposal—a concurrence essential to demission in the normal way. In the old days it presented very great difficulty indeed. Prior to 1933 the matter was covered in the former Church of Scotland by what was known as 'the Belhaven Act' and in the United Free Church by an Act of their Assembly of 1904. Since there is today no minister in a charge who was inducted thereto prior to June 1933, these are matters of purely historic interest.

The situation today is governed by the Act of 1933 whose provisions briefly are as follows. When a Presbytery is satisfied on the strength of soul-and-conscience certificates from two independent doctors that the minister of one of its charges is by reason of mental illness no longer fit to discharge his duties, it is to appoint an Interim Moderator to the Kirk Session concerned. If the incapacity looks to be of a temporary character leave of absence for a suitable period is to be given. If it appears that no improvement is to be expected, or if after a year there is still no immediate prospect of recovery, the Presbytery is to refer the matter to the General Assembly which may dissolve the pastoral tie, and which if it does so will arrange that suitable provision be made for the minister concerned—any such grants to be reviewable should he recover sufficiently to undertake ministerial or other duty of a remunerative nature.

Index

When the page-number is printed in italics this means that at that point the subject receives some fairly substantial treatment, the others may be passing references.